Essence of the Supreme Reality

Abhinavagupta's Paramārthasāra

AVAILABLE WITH ORIGINAL
VIDEO OR AUDIO MATERIAL

Revealed by

Swami Lakshmanjoo

John Hughes, Editor

Lakshmanjoo Academy

Published by:

Lakshmanjoo Academy

First printing 2010

Printed in the United States of America

For information, address:
Lakshmanjoo Academy
http://www.lakshmanjooacademy.org

ISBN 978-0-9837833-5-0 (paperback)
ISBN 978-0-9837833-9-8 (hardcover)

This pursuit is dedicated to Swami Lakshmanjoo
to whom we owe everything.

Table of Contents

Guide to Pronunciation

The following English words exemplify the pronunciation of selected Saṅskṛit vowels and consonants. The Romanized Saṅskṛit vowel or consonant is first listed and then an English word is given to aid you in its proper pronunciation.

a	as	a in ***A***merica.
ā	as	a in f***a***ther.
i	as	i in f***i***ll, l***i***ly.
ī	as	i in pol***i***ce.
u	as	u in f***u***ll.
ū	as	u in r***u***de.
ṛi	as	ri in mer***ri***ly.
ṛī	as	ri in ma***ri***ne.
e	as	e in pr***e***y.
ai	as	ai in ***ai***sle.
o	as	o in st***o***ne.
au	as	ou in h***ou***se
ś	as	s in ***s***ure.
ṣ	as	sh in ***sh***un, bu***sh***
s	as	s in ***s***aint, ***s***un

Preface

It is well-founded that the original author of the Paramārthasāra was Adiśeṣa, who Swamiji Lakshmanjoo affirms to be none other than the illustrious Muni Patañjali, author of the Yoga Sūtras. Considered to be a Vaiṣṇavite text consisting of some 85 verses, Abhinavagupta expanded upon Patañjali's original by changing the text here and there and including an additional 20 verses. As Swamiji says, "Abhinavagupta gave the Paramārthasāra a whitewash of Shaivism." In his recension of the Paramārthasāra, Abhinavagupta encapsulates the core teachings of the more formidable Kashmiri Shaiva works such as his voluminous Tantrāloka and Utpaladeva's Iśvarapratyabhijñā.

In the Spring of 1990, Swami Lakshmanjoo translated Abhinavagupta's Paramārthasāra[1] ("The Essence of the Supreme Reality"). The Paramārthasāra was one of the last texts he revealed before leaving his body, the others being the Bhagavad Gītā and the Stavacintāmaṇi.[2] The Paramārthasāra and the Bhagavad Gītā are the only two lecture series of Swamiji that we have recorded on video. During his translation of the 6th chapter of the Bhagavad Gītā, Swamiji intimated that, in 1989, he had experienced a profound and consummate spiritual transformation in which he realized the supreme state of Universal God consciousness. He emphatically declared to us, "I am Parabhairava!"[3] Swamiji's explanation of the Bhagavad Gītā, Paramārthasāra, and the Stavacintāmaṇi are clearly infused with the

---

1 The text which Swamiji used was the *Kashmir Series of Texts and Studies* (*KSTS*) Vol. VII, *The Paramārthasāra by Abhinavagupta*, with commentary of Yogarāja. This book has copious hand written notes by Swamiji, which have been added as footnotes in this publication.

2 Unfortunately, the video recording of the *Stavacintāmaṇi* was lost after a theft in Nepal. Fortunately, Denise Hughes took copious notes during Swamiji's revelation of this text.

3 See *Paramārthasāra* verses 10 and 11 for Swamiji's explanation of Parabhairava (the Absolute).

nectar of his beatific realization.

This is the second edition of Swami Lakshmanjoo's translation of the Paramārthasāra with Yogarāja's commentary. Though the first edition, published in 2010, was also based on the original recordings (1990), this present edition has been expanded in the way of additional footnotes, a comprehensive appendix, a bibliography, and an index. The quality of the original DVD recordings have also been enhanced, and subtitles have also been included.

I was first introduced to the text of the Paramārthasāra in 1972 while studying for my doctorate in Religious Studies at McMasters University, in Hamilton, Ontario. My teacher, Professor J.G. Arapura, was excited about the fact that I had previously met Swami Lakshmanjoo (1969), and that that meeting, though brief as it was, had kindled in me a desire to study the relatively unknown philosophy of Kashmir Shaivism.

I had always wanted to study under a real yogi, a person who lived his spiritual tradition, rather than going to a college or a university and studying in the dryness of a lecture hall. As Swami Lakshmanjoo had already gained international reputation as a scholar, saint, and advanced yogi in the discipline of Kashmir Shaivism, he was well-respected in the scholarly community, which was unusual for yogis in India. So, I received funds from the university along with their permission to travel to Kashmir and study at the feet of this great master.

Along with my wife, Denise, and my two year old daughter, Shanna, we reached Swami Lakshmanjoo's ashram in the winter of 1971-72. My first formal meeting with Swamiji was the greatest turning point in my life. Swamiji greeted me warmly and immediately reached into his pocket and produced a picture of my family that I had previously sent. With warmth and affection he said, "I have been waiting for you." This was just a profound experience for me and I told him, "I know you are God and I am here to study with you and to be with you."

Swamiji agreed that he would teach me Kashmir Shaivism, and that was the start of a wonderful adventure for myself and my family. From the start, I began recording all of his lectures, and soon he indicated that he was pleased with my assimilation of his teachings. After some time, it became clear that Swamiji was concerned about the future of his tradition. He felt that if his teachings were not properly preserved, they would be lost once he left this world. After all, he was the last living exponent of the 'Oral Tradition of Kashmir Shaivism'.

One day, Swamiji asked me if I would be interested in continuing to study and record his translations of what he considered to be the most important texts of Kashmir Shaivism. He was keenly interested that this knowledge should be preserved and made available for mankind. I felt honored that this great master and saint considered me worthy of such an important undertaking, so, instead of going back to finish my thesis, I decided to stay in Kashmir along with my wife and my daughter. For the next fifteen years, Swamiji taught us the essence of Kashmir Shaivism through his translations and explanations of his selections of sacred texts. As a result, we accumulated over 700 hours of recordings of Swamiji's English translations along with many hours of his lectures in the Kashmiri language.

In the beginning, I continued to work on Abhinavagupta's recension of the Paramārthasāra with the idea that I would eventually complete my thesis. With the shifted focus of recording and studying other important texts under Swamiji, I found little time for this project. As a result, my unfinished thesis sat idle for these past 43 years. Still, almost half a century later, I am thankful for the help I received from Lalita Dhar for her contribution to my work on this text. In hindsight, I realize that time is never lost while studying this profound tradition. So, to give further clarification to this present publication, I have drawn upon my original manuscript in the form of footnotes and have also included a literal translation of all of the 106 verses (see Appendix B). Upon completion of his final lecture of this Paramārthasāra, Swamiji handed me his own manuscript which contained many of his handwritten notes. These precious notes have been included as footnotes throughout the text.

Unlike other Kashmir Shaiva treatises, Abhinavagupta's

Paramārthasāra does not indulge in stringent dialectic or terse logical argumentation. Rather, it is a straightforward piece intended primarily for novices, yet highly beneficial even for the more advanced Trika[4] practitioner.

Jai Guru Dev !

John Hughes
April 15, 2015

4 "*Trika*" means, trinity, a group of three. Trika Shaivism is the three-fold science of man and his world.

Acknowledgements

First of all, I would like to thank my wife Denise, my son Viresh, my daughter Shanna, George Barselaar, Claudia Dose, Stephen Benson, and Michael Van Winkle, all of whom made the success of this project possible. They all proved to be invaluable in the preparation of the transcript and videos for the publication of this *Paramārthasāra*. To George van den Barselaar for his untiring dedication in preparing the original transcript. To Stephen Benson for his masterful editing. To my son Viresh for adding numerous footnotes and appendix for clarification of the text. To Michael Van Winkle, our audio engineer, who utilized a number of tricks and techniques to polish, clarify, and enhance the original audio. To Claudia Dose, our creative director, who typed the *Devanāgarī* and was responsible for creating the look and feel of the DVD, its menus, structure, and interface. To Shanna, who managed all aspects of the project, tirelessly working to have it completed in a timely manner. And finally, to Denise for her proofing (nothing was approved without her nod). She watched the videos and listened to the audio and made many valuable editing suggestions.

Swami Lakshmanjoo

Swami Lakshmanjoo

The Author

Swami Lakshmanjoo was born in Srinagar, Kashmir, on May 9, 1907. He was the most recent and the greatest of the long line of saints and masters of the Kashmir Shaiva tradition. From his early childhood, Swamiji spent his life studying and practicing the teachings of this unique and sacred tradition. Having a complete intellectual and spiritual understanding of the philosophy and practice of Kashmir Shaivism, he was a true master in every respect.

Being born with a photographic memory, learning was always easy for him. In addition to possessing a complete knowledge of Kashmir Shaivism, he had a vast knowledge of the traditional religious and philosophical schools and texts of India. Swamiji would freely draw upon other texts to clarify, expand, and substantiate his lectures. He could recall an entire text by simply remembering the first few words of a verse.

In time, his reputation as a learned philosopher and spiritual adept spread. Spiritual leaders and scholars journeyed from all over the world to receive his blessings and to ask him questions about various aspects of Kashmir Shaiva philosophy. He gained renown as a devotee of Lord Shiva and as a master of the nondual tradition of Kashmir Shaivism.

Throughout his life, Swamiji taught his disciples and devotees the ways of devotion and awareness. He shunned fame and recognition and did not seek his own glory. He knew Kashmir

Shaivism was the most precious jewel and that, by God's grace, those who desired supreme knowledge would be attracted to its teachings. His earnest wish was for Kashmir Shaivism to be preserved and made available to all humankind.

In 1990, during his stay in Nepal, Swamiji translated Abhinavagupta's unique commentaries on the *Paramārthasāra* and the *Bhagavad Gītā*. During his explanation of the sixth chapter of the *Bhagavad Gītā*, Swamiji gave a rare glimpse into the fullness and glory of his own experience:

> I was smoothly going on with my practice and abruptly *śaktipāta* (grace) came and threw all its force in me. It was *tīvra tīvra* (super-supreme) *śaktipāta*. And then it happened and I was newborn. I became so great. I don't mean to boast but this is what happened. I was newly reborn. And, because I had to become Bhairava, I had to experience all of the states of *yoga*. And it happened, everything happened. I had all experiences; and *cidānanda* also, *jagadānanda*[5] also. Everything happened. You can't imagine the ways of *śaktipāta*.[6]

On the 27th of September, 1991, Swami Lakshmanjoo left his physical body and attained *mahasamādhi*, the great liberation.

---

5 *Cidānanda* and *jagadānanda* are the final stages of the seven states of *tūrya*, also known as the seven states of *ānanda* (bliss). See *Kashmir Shaivism, The Secret Supreme*, 16.113-115.

6 Bhagavd Gītā in the Light of Kashmir Śhaivism DVD 6.3 (42:01). For complete explanation of *śaktipāta* see appendix 7.

YOGARAJA'S INTRODUCTION

SWAMIJI: Let us start [with] his *śloka* at the beginning of the commentary, his commentary, i.e., Yogarāja's[1].

PS DVD 1 (0:00:08)

चिद्घनोऽपि जगन्मूर्त्या
श्यानो यः स जयत्यजः ।
स्वात्मप्रच्छादनक्रीडा
विदग्धः परमेश्वरः ॥१॥

cidghano'pi jaganmūrtyā[2]
śyāno yaḥ sa jayatyajaḥ /
svātmapracchādanakrīḍā-
vidagdhaḥ parameśvaraḥ //1//

Cidghano'pi parameśvaraḥ, although Parameśvara, Lord Śiva, is *cid ghana*, filled with all-consciousness, but *yaḥ jagat mūrtyā śyāna*, who has taken the formation of the universe and He is coagulated there.[3] [The universe] is the coagulated formation of *cid ghana*.

The consciousness of the Lord is just rubbery. You know "rubbery" [laughter]? It is liquid form and It has frozen. The frozen

1 Yogarāja was a direct disciple of Kṣemarāja, who was the chief disciple of Abhinavagupta.

2 "That Bhairava who is never born and never the victim of death." (Swami Lakshmanjoo's handwritten notes)

3 "Although *caitanyarūpa**, always, no matter if He has taken the formation of the universe and seems to be coagulated, [He is] not actually coagulated." Ibid. *The embodiment of completely independent consciousness.

state of that *cid ghana* is this universe. This is also good! Yogarāja says that this universe is the frozen state of Lord Śiva whose consciousness, Self-consciousness, universal consciousness, is coagulated. It has become . . .

JONATHAN: It mats together.

SWAMIJI: Yes.

And *svātma pracchādana krīḍāvidagdhaḥ*, the main purpose of Lord Śiva is just to show the playful trick of hiding[4], how He hides His real nature. He has hidden His real nature in the manifestation of the world. In the manifestation of the world, He is hidden. Otherwise, He is also there.

PS DVD 1 (0:02:33)

योऽयं व्यधायि गुरुणा
युक्त्या परमार्थसारसंक्षेपः।
विवृतिं करोमि लघ्वीम्
अस्मिन् विद्वज्जनार्थितो योगः ॥२॥

yo'yaṁ vyadhāyi guruṇā
yuktyā paramārthasārasaṁkṣepaḥ /
vivṛtiṁ karomi laghvīm
asmin vidvajjanārthito yogaḥ //2//

This *paramārthasāra saṁkṣepaḥ*, the essence[5] of the *Paramārthasāra*, which was described by Śeṣa Patañjali[6] to his disciple, his essence was revealed, penned down, by our great grand-teacher of teachers, Abhinavagupta[7]. He has penned down the essence of that *Paramārthasāra*, which was sometime, in olden ancient times, related to some disciple by lord Patañjali.

---

4 "By His own trick." (Swami Lakshmanjoo's handwritten notes)

5 "Essence or cream." Ibid.

6 Patañjali is variously referred to as Lord Patañjali, Ādiśeṣa Patañjali, Patañjali Muni, or Śeṣa Muni.

7 Abhinavagupta was the teacher of Kṣemarāja, who in turn was the teacher of Yogarāja. Hence, Abhinavagupta was Yogarāja's grand-teacher.

JOHN: The same Patañjali as the *Yoga Sūtras* Patañjali?

SWAMIJI: Yes.

In that, I[8] am taking the effort of doing the commentary on those *ślokas* of Abhinavagupta.

Bas[9], these [introductory *ślokas* are finished]. Now, Abhinavagupta's *śloka*:

8 Yogarāja.

9 A Hindi expression frequently used by Swamiji, which literally means "that is all" or "enough", often signifies the end of a topic or a train of thought.

PARAMĀRTHASĀRA of ABHINAVAGUPTA

PS DVD 1 (00:04:20)

परं परस्थं गहनाद् अनादिम्
एकं निविष्टं बहुधा गुहासु ।
सर्वालयं सर्वचराचरस्थं
त्वामेव शांभुं शरणं प्रपद्ये ॥ १ ॥

paraṁ parasthaṁ gahanād anādim
ekaṁ niviṣṭaṁ bahudhā guhāsu /
sarvālayaṁ sarvacarācarasthaṁ
tvāmeva śaṁbhuṁ śaraṇaṁ prapadye //1//

Param. Who is *param*? *Param* means filled with the five energies: *cit*, *ānanda*, *icchā*, *jñāna*, and *kriyā*. You know these five energies? That is *param*. *Param* means *pūrṇam*, who is filled with five energies.[10]

Gahanād parastham, who is above *māyā*, who is situated above (*gahanāt* means *māyā*[11]); *anādim*, who has no beginning; *ekam*, who is one; and who has *niviṣṭam*, who has entered in various caves of the heart of universality. He has entered in the cave of Parabhairava. He has entered in the cave of . . . just like

10 He has got five energies: *cit śakti* (energy of consciousness), *ānanda śakti* (energy of bliss), *icchā śakti* (energy of will), *jñāna śakti* (energy of knowledge), and *kriyā śakti* (energy of action).

11 "*Māyā śakti* is that universal energy, which is owned by individual being, individual soul. The same energy, when it is owned by universal being, is called *svātantrya śakti*." Swami Lakshmanjoo, *Kashmir Shaivism–The Secret Supreme* (Universal Shaiva Fellowship, Los Angeles, 2000). For explanation of *svātantrya śakti* see Appendix A-2.

from Parabhairava[12] to the heart of a neglected insect. He has entered in that, in the heart of an insect also, and He has entered in the heart of Paramaśiva also.

Sarvālayam, He is *viśrānti*, the abode of everybody. All are resting in That.[13] *Sarva carācarastham*, and who is where all *jaḍa* (inert) and *cetana* (conscious) classes are resting.[14]

I bow to Thee, O Śiva, and *śaraṇam prapadye*, I bow to Thee and get entry in Your state for good.[15]

Next *śloka*:

PS DVD 1 (00:06:56)

गर्भाधिवासपूर्वक-
मरणान्तकदुः खचक्रविभ्रान्तः ।
आधारं भगवन्तं
शिष्यः पप्रच्छ परमार्थम् ॥२॥

आधारकारिकाभिः
तं गुरुरभिभाषते स्म तत्सारम् ।
कथयत्यभिनवगुप्तः
शिवशासनदृष्टियोगेन ॥३॥

garbhādhivāsapūrvaka-
maraṇāntakaduḥ khacakravibhrāntaḥ /
ādhāraṁ bhagavantaṁ
śiṣyaḥ papraccha paramārthaṁ //2//

12 Parabhairava is synonymous with Paramaśiva (supreme Śiva), the state of universal God consciousness. See also commentary verses 10-11.

13 "He alone is manifested in the worldly field." (Swami Lakshmanjoo's handwritten notes)

14 "Thus Lord Bhairava is found in each and every form, and, at the same time, His being formlessness also cannot be denied." Ibid.

15 "I become one, diluted in Thee." Ibid.

ādhārakārikābhiḥ
taṁ gururabhibhāṣate smatatsāram /
kathayatyabhinavaguptaḥ
śivaśāsanadṛṣṭiyogena //3//

Kaścit śiṣyaḥ, some disciple, some particular disciple . . . *Ādhāraṁ bhagavantaṁ, paramārthaṁ papraccha. Ādhāraṁ bhagavantaṁ*, Śeṣamuni (Patañjali), who was the founder of the *Yoga Sūtras*, and the *Yoga Sūtras* were commentated upon by Patañjali . . .[16]

PS DVD 1 (00:08:14)

योगेन चित्तस्य पदेन वाचा
मलम् शरीरस्य तु वैद्यकेनम् ।
योऽपाकरोत्तं प्रवरं मुनीनाम्
पतञ्जलिर्प्राञ्जलिरानतोऽस्मीम् ॥

yogena cittasya padena vācā
malam śarīrasya tu vaidyakenam /
yo'pākarottaṁ pravaraṁ munīnām
patañjalirprāñjalirānato'smīm //[17]

Yogena cittasya malam. Patañjali discarded the *mala* of mind, the impurity of the mind, by *yoga*. Because the *yoga darśaṇa*[18] he has also penned down–the *yoga darśaṇa*. By the *yoga darśaṇa*, he has removed, he has destroyed, the

16 "The disciple, bewildered by the wheel of suffering which begins with life in the womb and ends in death, asks the guru, blesssed Ādhāra (Patañjali) for truth." *Paramārthasāra*, with Yogarājas commentary, translated by John Hughes, Ishwar Ashram, Srinagar, Kashmir. (PhD. thesis, McMasters University, Hamilton, Ontario, 1972.)

17 Showing respect for Patañjali, the author of the *Paramārthasāra*, Swamiji recited this verse from the *Bhojavṛtti*, i.e., Bhoja's commentary on Patañjali's *Yoga Sūtras*. Swamiji's recitation differs slightly from the standard. Note: This verse does not appear in the text of the *Paramārthasāra*.

18 The *Yoga Sūtras*.

impurity of the mind–by the *yoga darśaṇa*, by *yoga* (*yogena cittasya*).
Padena vācā, by grammar he has destroyed the *mala* (impurity) of, the behavior of, *vāk* (speech). When the Sanskrit language is correct, it means he is well-scholarly qualified in Sanskrit grammar. And he has commentated upon that also. And, by that, he has succeeded [in] discarding the impurity of speech–[by] speaking in Sanskrit.
When Hanumān bowed before Rāma and spoke to Him in the Sanskrit language, Rāma was so highly overjoyed to see that, [by] his grammar, he was a very learned scholar. Who?

DENISE: Hanumān.

SWAMIJI: Hanumān.
[Rāma] said, "[Hanumān's] behavior of talk is just like the behavior of the gods. He is a godly man. He can do and undo everything for Me. He has been created by God for Me, to help Me in finding out [My] lost wife [who] was snatched away by Rāvaṇa[19] [laughter]".

yogena cittasya padena vācā
malam śarīrasya tu vaidyakenam / [repeated]

And [Patañjali] has also done Vaidika (Vaidika means this philosophy of diseases). The philosophy of diseases, it is Vaidika literature. That is called Caraka.[20] It is in the *Vedās* also.

DENISE: Āyurvedic?

SWAMIJI: Āyurvedic, yes. The Āyurvedic literature, he has commentated upon. No, he has created that! He is the author of that book where that treatment for all diseases are

19 The demon Rāvaṇa and his brother, Kumbhakarṇa, were incarnations of Lord Viṣṇu's beloved guards, Jaya and Vijaya. The demon Rāvaṇa is revered throughout India as Lord Śiva's greatest devotee. [*Editor's note*]

20 The *Caraka Saṁhitā* is one of three classical texts of Āyurveda. [*Editor's note*]

explained[21]. This treatment is for that disease, this treatment is for [another] disease, and this is how you should get the pulse rate and everything, and whatever diseases you find in the body, those will be [cured], but [only by the] Vaidic [treatment].

So, that *pravaraṁ munīnām*, he who is the greatest of all the great *ṛṣis* (Patañjali), I bow before him; Patañjali who is the creator of all these three sections: *yoga*, and speech, and disease (the removal of all diseases).

Tat sāram kathayati abhinavaguptaḥ. "And that *Paramārthasāra* is placed by Abhinavagupta, me, myself, . . ."

It is Abhinavagupta's saying, Abhinavagupta's writing. He calls him[self] as Abhinavagupta.

". . . and I am here placing the essence of all that knowledge which was explained to his *śiṣya* (disciple) by Patañjali. But I give it a whitewash of Shaivism, I will give you a whitewash of Shaivism. In a Shaivite way, I will describe that."[22]

[Three] *ślokas* are finished.[23]

PS DVD 1 (00:14:44)

निजशक्तिवैभवभराद्
अण्डचतुष्टयमिदं विभागेन ।
शक्तिर्माया प्रकृतिः
पृथ्वी चेति प्रभावितं प्रभुणा ॥४॥

21 Patañjali is recognized by many scholars to be one of the authors of the *Caraka Saṁhita*. According to some, Patañjali is said to be the sage Caraka himself. [*Editor's note*]

22 "And afterwards, its cream, Abhinavagupta explains according to the viewpoint of Shaivism. [That *Paramārthasāra*] becomes very great by the viewpoint of Trika." (Swami Lakshmanjoo's handwritten notes)

23 "Now, how this universe is manifested; why and with which purpose Bhairava (Śiva) lays its foundation. By His supermost unobjectionable *svātantrya*, He manifests the universe . . . just to make the reader understand that this universe is just the expansion of His energies." Ibid.

nija-śakti-vaibhava-bharād
aṇḍa-catuṣṭayam-idaṁ vibhāgena /
śaktir-māyā prakṛtiḥ
pṛthvī ceti prabhāvitaṁ prabhuṇā //4//

Prabhuṇa, Lord Śiva, has *prabhāvitam* (created) four *aṇḍas* (four circles) of this universe: *śaktyaṇḍa*, *māyāṇḍa*, *prakṛtyaṇḍa*, and *pṛthvyaṇḍa*. *Pṛthvī-aṇḍa* is the lowest circle, and outside that there is another circle which is called *prakṛti-aṇḍa*. Outside that *prakṛti-aṇḍā*, there is another circle which is called *māyā-aṇḍa*. Outside that [*māyā-aṇḍa*], there is a circle which is called *śakti-aṇḍa*.

So, there are these four circles: . . .

JOHN: They're egg-shaped circles, are they not?

SWAMIJI: . . . *nivṛtti kalā*, *pratiṣṭhā kalā*, *vidyā kalā*, and *śānta kalā*. *Nivṛtti kalā* is the first, and outside that is *pratiṣṭhā kalā*, and outside that is *vidyā kalā*, and outside that is *śānta kalā*. These *kalās* are greater than each other. And the fifth is *śāntā*[*tītā*] *kalā*. *Nivṛtti kalā*, *pratiṣṭhā kalā*, *vidyā kalā*, and *śānta kalā*, and the fifth is *śāntātītā kalā*.[24]

In *śāntātītā kalā*, there are no worlds (*śāntātītā tvabhuvan-aiva*); *śāntātītā kalā* is without any world. There is no world, there is only the glamour of Lord Śiva. There is no residence of anybody [else], this is only the residence of Lord Śiva.

JOHN: These are egg-shaped circles.

SWAMIJI: Huh?

JOHN: These circles. *Aṇḍa* means "egg-shaped".

SWAMIJI: Egg-shaped, yes.

JOHN: Why does he call them "egg-shaped"? Why are they egg-shaped? Why not round? Why egg-shaped?

SWAMIJI: Because it is an egg, it is creative, it has to create, it has got creative strength. It creates, so it is an egg. It is just like an egg (*aṇḍa*).

---

24 *Nivṛtti kalā*, *pratiṣṭhā kalā*, *vidyā kalā*, and *śānta kalā* are also known as *pṛthvyaṇḍa*, *prakṛtyaṇḍa*, *māyāṇḍa*, and *śaktyaṇḍa*, respectively. For an explanation of the five *kalās*, see Appendix A-8.

Vastupiṇḍo'ṇḍamucyate[25], *aṇḍa* is that, the egg is that, where there is so much existing in undifferentiated form. For instance, there is the egg of a peacock. That is also a white [substance] in the egg, but you will find so many colors in that [peacock], all colors.

JOHN: The whole existence of the peacock is in that one white [substance].

SWAMIJI: Yes. In the same way, everything is white there, but, at the time of expanding into manifestation, these colors appear separately.

JOHN: *Saṅkoca* and *vikāsa*.

SWAMIJI: *Saṅkoca* and *vikāsa.*[26] *Saṅkoca* is in seed form, *vikāsa* is in manifestation.

Pṛthvī, *prakṛti*, *māyā*, and *śakti*, He has created it not for any purpose. He was craving . . . He was mad about His too much of *ānanda* (ecstasy, bliss). When there is too much of *ānanda*, you jump and go and drown in . . . you want to finish your body when you cannot tolerate that too much ecstasy of your being. When too much ecstasy of [your] being is overflowing, then you lose your wits. You cannot remain in that position, in your own position. You want to manifest outside also. When you are stuck inside, [you scream], "*haaaaaaaaaaaa*" [laughter]. When you are . . .

DENISE: Explode.

SWAMIJI: Yes, you want to expose everything to everybody!

Nija śakti vaibhava bharāt, when the glamour of His own energies (*cit śakti*, *ānanda śakti*, *icchā śakti*, *jñāna śakti*, and *kriyā śakti*) are overflowing, overflowing with glamour, He creates this universe. This is the creation because He was overflowing in His way, in His being.[27]

---

25 Yogarāja's commentary.

26 Contraction and expansion, respectively.

27 "Look at [a child]. When he is too much excited, he jumps, he hits his head. In the same way, God has done this. He has crushed His own nature because of too much ecstasy. He wants to disconnect that ecstasy. But that ecstasy in its real way cannot be disconnected at all. He knows that. But still, for fun, He disconnects this for the time being. And at the time of again realizing His own nature, He feels that it was

PS DVD 1 (00:20:56)

तत्रान्तर्विश्वमिदं
विचित्रतनु-करण-भुवनसंतानम् ।
भोक्ता च तत्र देही
शिव एव गृहीतपशुभावः ॥५॥

tatrāntar-viśvam-idaṁ
vicitra-tanu-karaṇa bhuvanam-saṁtānam /
bhoktā ca tatra dehī
śiva eva gṛhīta-paśu-bhāvaḥ / /5/ /

Tatra āntar viśvam idaṁ. *Tatra*, in those four *aṇḍas*, four egg-shaped circles, is existing this whole universe.[28] And, in which universe, *vicitratanu karaṇa bhuvanaṁ satānam*, the bodies are different from each other, and *karaṇa*, the organs are different.

It is not always that you can see [only] with the eyes. You can see with this skin also, you can hear with the nostrils also, you can smell with taste [i.e., the tongue] also.[29]

Bhoktā ca tatra dehī, in these five circles, the enjoyer is *dehī*[30],

---

already there." Swami Lakshmanjoo, *Bodhapañcadaśikā*, USF archive.

28 "These . . . are not other than Śiva." (Swami Lakshmanjoo's hand-written notes)

29 "It is explained by Aniruddha, [one] master of Abhinavagupta. *Mukhyataḥ tatsthāne vṛittimanti*, but, in the ordinary way, they act in their own place in hands, i.e., the action of holding lies in the hands in predominance. But [this capacity] is not always lying in the hand. Otherwise, when the hand is crippled, when the hand is cut, [the holding] action is still there. You can hold with some other organ–with the mouth, or with the elbow, or with the foot. For instance, I see through my eyes but I can feel also the sensation of seeing without the eyes. When I am absolutely blind, I can feel the sensation of form. I can feel the sensation of smell without the nose. I can feel the sensation of touch without the skin. I can feel the sensation of taste without the tongue, and so on." Swami Lakshmanjoo, *Tantrāloka* 9.260-267, USF archive.

30 The body-holder.

the limited being.[31] Which limited being? *Siva eva*, Lord Siva Himself, but who has taken the formation of a limited being, *jīva*, the limited soul.[32] Lord Śiva is enjoying this.

PS DVD 1 (00:22:49)

नानाविधवर्णानां
    रूपं धत्ते यथाऽमलः स्फटिकः ।
सुरमानुषपशुपादप-
    रूपत्वं तद्वदीशोऽपि ॥६॥

nānā-vidha-varṇānāṁ
    rūpaṁ dhatte yathā'malaḥ sphaṭikaḥ /
sura-mānuṣa-paśu-pādapa-
    rūpatvaṁ tad-vadīśo'pi //6//

Nānāvidha varṇānāṁ rūpaṁ, just as (*yathā*, just as) *amala sphaṭika*, glittering, that *sphaṭika manī*, a kind of jewel, which is called . . .

DENISE: Diamond.

SWAMIJI: Not diamond. *Sphaṭika*, that crystal, [it] takes the face of all colors. All colors shine in that crystal. *Nānāvidhavarṇānāṁ rūpaṁ dhatte yathā amalaḥ*, if it is properly cleaned, that crystal takes on the reflection of all colors–in *sphaṭika*.

. . . in the same way–this is an example–in the same way, *tadvat īśo'pi*, Bhagavān Bhairava (Lord Bhairava) also *sura*, takes the formation of *devās* (gods), takes the formation of limited beings (*paśu*), takes the formation of . . .

Paśu means "beasts".

. . . *pādapa*, takes the formation of trees, and all these forma-

---

31 "All 118 worlds, 36 elements, and 5 *kalās* are residing in one's body." Swami Lakshmanjoo, *Tantrāloka* 16.99, USF archive.

32 "Actually, Lord Bhairava has possessed the state of limitation and seems to be an ignorant soul." (Swami Lakshmanjoo's handwritten notes)

tions He takes just like *sphaṭika manī* (crystal jewel). He becomes everything. He has taken the formation of all these worldly objects.[33]

PS DVD 1 (00:25:08)

गच्छति गच्छति जल इव
हिमकरबिम्बं स्थिते स्थितिं याति ।
तनु-करण-भुवनवर्गे
तथाऽयमात्मा महेशानः ॥७॥

gacchati gacchati jala iva
hima-kara-bimbaṁ sthite sthitiṁ yāti /
tanu-karaṇa-bhuvana-varge
tathā'yam-ātmā maheśānaḥ //7//

Just as *himakarabimbaṁ*, the reflection of . . .

Himakara means "who has got very cold light". Who has got cold light?

JONATHAN: The moon.

SWAMIJI: *Shabash*[34]!

. . . that, the cold light of the moon, just as *gacchati jala* (one *gacchati* is *saptami*[35]), in a moving pool, a moving stream, water, when the water is moving, in moving water, when the water is flowing, this stream of water is flowing, in that, [when] the reflection of the moon takes [its] reflection in that, and in that one can find that this is moving (the moon is moving in that moving water), and when the reflection of the moon is seen in stable water, in a pool, the moon seems, *bas*, as stable, it does not move there, but, actually, neither it moves nor it does not move, in the same way, *tanu karaṇa bhuvana varge*, when Lord Śiva

33 "It is Bhairava who has become the gods, individuals, beasts, and even trees, stones, etc., and is in fact not away from His divine nature." (Swami Lakshmanjoo's handwritten notes)

"Lord Śiva is the victim of repeated births and deaths." Ibid.

34 Hindi for "bravo" or "kudos".

35 Lit., the seventh case (locative).

takes the formation of the body, when Lord Siva takes the formation of the organs, when Lord Śiva takes the formation of the worlds, He becomes just [like] the body, He becomes just like the organs, He becomes just like the worlds. He has taken the formation of the worlds, He has taken the formation of the body, He has taken the formation of the organs. He has taken the formation [of everything].[36]

That [analogy of the moon] was an example. This is the reality of Lord Śiva. He has taken all these formations.

PS DVD 1 (00:28:25)

राहुरदृश्योऽपि यथा
  शशिबिम्बस्थः प्रकाशते, तद्वत् ।
सर्वगतोऽप्ययमात्मा
  विषयाश्रयणेन धीमुकुरे ॥८॥

rāhur-adṛśyo'pi yathā
  śaśi-bimba-sthaḥ prakāśate tadvat /
sarva-gato'pyayam-ātmā
  viśayāśrayaṇena dhī-mukure //8//

Rāhu, just like Rāhu (Rāhu means Rāhu, that eclipse), *adṛśy-o'pi yathā*, although he is residing in *ākaśa*[37]–Rāhu is in *ākāśa* always–*adṛśya*, but he is not observed by anybody . . .*

He is observed only at the time of the eclipse (the moon eclipse or the sun eclipse) because the moon and the sun come in his way. Rāhu is going on [i.e., existing in] *ākāśa*.[38] Actually, his color

---

36 "Actually, when Lord Śiva is residing in a body, at that time also the body is dead; and when Lord Śiva comes out from the limited body, that body is still dead. So, in both ways, the body is dead and that possession of a body is His divine play." (Swami Lakshmanjoo's handwritten notes)

37 Ether, space.

38 When the gods churned this *kṣīra sāgara*, that milky ocean (*kṣīra samudrā*), and nectar came out of it by churning, and Lord Viṣṇu told all Gods that they can use this nectar and they [would] become immortal by drinking that nectar. So they began to drink it. This Rāhu, a demon in disguise of gods, came and began to drink this nectar also. A

is just like dark blue. He is residing in *ākāśa*, in dark blue, and he is just the color of *ākāśā*, so you cannot observe him. You can observe him only when it comes, just when *śaśi* (the moon) passes, *śaśi* goes on, moves in *ākāśa*, and it comes just in the [way of the sun]. That is in this position [Swamiji indicates].

JOHN: In the way.

SWAMIJI: In the way. And [then] you can see that it is Rāhu. And we see that Rāhu has eaten this moon, he has eaten this moon. [Actually], he has not eaten, he does not eat it; it comes in the same line. *Śaśi bimbasthaḥ*, when it comes in *śaśi bimba* or *sūrya bimba* (or *bimba* (reflection) of the sun), you can perceive that.

*. . . in the same way, *sarvagato'pyayamātmā*, [although] *ātma*[39] is always existing in the world, but *ātma* is held, you can behold *ātma*, only when there are organs, and there is intellect, and you [say], "I have got . . . I am hungry. I am weak. I have got a headache. I am happy. I am peaceful. I am nowhere. I am filled with grief". The individual says that. The individual says to his mother or to his friends that, "I am not well today". How he says that? He says [that] only because he is . . . he does not behold [the *ātma*] exactly, but he beholds it. And the *ātma* is supposed to be there (*ātma* means the "soul"), the soul seems to be there. With the existence of the soul, it seems that there is life in the organs. Otherwise, in the organs, in the body, there is no life. When the body is dead, you can't see anything.

Now [Abhinavagupta] says, "If the body is there, why Lord Śiva is only perceived in *samādhi*[40], not in this position?" In the

---

few drops he drunk and the Moon and Sun observed [that Rāhu] is a fraud, that he had come in disguise and drank this nectar. He had tasted only a few drops of that nectar but this was observed by the Moon and Sun. When the Moon and Sun both took this message to Viṣṇu (Nārāyaṇa), He cut [Rāhu's] head and separated it from his body. But as he had tasted this nectar, his head also remained alive, but he had this wrath against the the Moon and Sun. It is a tradition in our religion that he has this kind of wrath, this kind of enmity against the Sun and Moon. So he eats the Sun and Moon on the day of eclipses." Swami Lakshmanjoo, *Tantrāloka* 6.65, USF archive.

39 The soul or the self.

40 For an explanation of *samādhi*, see Appendix A-9.

ordinary position of the daily routine of life, you cannot perceive God as you perceive that God in *samādhi*. Why [do] people perceive God only in *samādhi* [and] not perceive [God] in the daily routine of their activities? There also is the existence of God. Why it is not understood properly? It is understood in negation.

Viresh tells you, "Mummy, I am hungry". It seems Viresh is hungry. He has got some power of understanding. But there is a difference between this kind of understanding and understanding your Self in *samādhi*. There is a difference in that.

He says, now he puts the question (it is [an understandable] question): "Why everybody does not go into *samādhi* when God is existing everywhere?" He says, "No, *samādhi* is only held by the *śaktipāta* (grace) of Lord Śiva".

PS DVD 1 (00:35:05)

आदर्शे मलरहिते
    यद्वद् वदनं विभाति तद्वद् अयम् ।
शिव-शक्तिपातविमले
    धीतत्त्वे भाति भारूपः ॥९॥

ādarśe mala-rahite
    yadvad vadanaṁ vibhāti tadvad ayam /
śiva-śakti-pāta-vimale
    dhī-tattve bhāti bhārūpaḥ //9//

Yadvad, just as *mala rahite ādarśe*, when a mirror is cleaned, is wiped off, from all dust and everything, it is pure, just as *vadanaṁ vibhāti*, your face shines exactly as you are–and you shave before that [mirror] with your razor and everything and all goes well–in the same way, *śivaśaktipāta vimale dhītattve*, when your intellectual power has become purified by the *tīvra-tīvra śaktipāta* of Lord Śiva[41], and then, in your intellectual under-

41 *Śaktipāta* literally means the descent of spiritual energy. "In the kingdom of spirituality, Lord Śiva creates masters and disciples through His fifth act, the act of grace (*anugraha*). This grace is ninefold and, therefore, He creates masters and disciples in nine different ways.

standing, you can perceive this position of Lord Siva in *samādhi* where you are supposed to be an elevated soul.[42]

So, being elevated or non-elevated, it has no meaning. It is only the play of Lord Śiva. When there is *śaktipāta*, you are elevated; when there is not *śaktipāta*, you are going on with your own [worldly] process, and that is also not separate from Lord Śiva's state.

PS DVD 1 (00:37:16)

भारूपं परिपूर्णं
    स्वात्मनि विश्रान्तितो महानन्दम् ।
इच्छासंवित्करणैर्
    निर्भरितम् अनन्तशक्तिपरिपूर्णम् ॥ १० ॥
सर्वविकल्पविहीनं
    शुद्धं शान्तं लयोदयविहीनम् ।
यत् परतत्त्वं तस्मिन्
    विभाति षट्त्रिंशदात्म जगत् ॥ ११ ॥

bhārūpaṁ paripūrṇaṁ
    svātmani viśrāntito mahānandam /
icchā-saṁvit-karaṇair
    nirbharitam ananta-śakti-paripūrṇam //10//
sarva-vikalpa-vihīnaṁ
    śuddhaṁ śāntaṁ layodaya-vihīnam /
yat para-tattvaṁ tasmin
    vibhāti ṣaṭ-triṁśad-ātma jagat //11//

Yat paratattvaṁ, that *para tattva*, that supreme element of

The first and highest level of grace is called *tīvra-tīvra śaktipāta.*" See *Kashmir Shaivism–The Secret Supreme*, 10.65-70. For more on *śaktipāta* (grace), see Appendix A-7.

42 "*Dhītattve*, that intellect is considered to be absolutely clear to observe one's own state of Bhairava." (Swami Lakshmanjoo's handwritten notes)

Lord Siva. That is the supreme element. That is, *para tattva* means exactly Parabhairava.

Now, the qualification of Parabhairava is described by Abhinavagupta in these two *ślokas*, the tenth and the eleventh.

bhārūpaṁ paripūrṇaṁ
svātmani viśrāntito mahānandam /
icchā-saṁvit-karaṇair
nirbharitam ananta-śakti-paripūrṇam //10//
[repeated]

Bhārupam, who is *bhārupam*, i.e., who is *prakāśa*, who is filled with *prakāśa*[43]; who is *paripūrṇam*, who is *pūrṇam* (full); *svātmani viśrāntito mahānandam*, who is residing in His own way and is filled with *ānanda* (bliss), the blissful state.

Bhārūpaṁ pari pūrnaṁ is, [He] who is *cit*, who is the embodiment of *cit śakti*[44]. *Svātmani viśrāntito mahānandam*, when He resides in His *cit śakti*, He becomes filled with *ānanda*.

Icchā saṁvit karaṇair, icchā nirbharitam. He is also filled with *icchā śakti*, *saṁvit* (*jñāna śakti*), and *karaṇair* (*kriyā śakti*). *Icchā* means the energy of will, *saṁvit* means the energy of knowledge, and *karaṇair* means the energy of action. He is filled with these three energies.

So, He is filled with *cit śakti*, *ānanda śakti*, *icchā śakti*, *jñāna śakti*, and *kriyā śakti*. And, exclusively, He is *ananta śakti paripūrṇam*, He is not only filled with the five energies, He has got numberless *śaktis*, numberless *śaktis*. *Ananta śakti paripūrṇam*, He is filled with all energies, which are offshoots of these five energies.

Sarva vikalpa vihīnaṁ, who is *sarva vikalpa vihīnaṁ*, all varieties of thoughts have taken their end there[45]; *śuddhaṁ*, who is clean; *śāntaṁ*, who is appeased; *layodaya vihīnam*, who is absent from rise and fall (He neither rises nor falls down). And

43 *Prakāśa* is the supreme light of God consciousness. For an explanation of *prakāśa*, see Appendix A-10.

44 The energy (*śakti*) of consciousness (*cit*).

45 "Unlimited thought is not thought, it is *nirvikalpa*. It is the state of your own nature where there is no limitation." Swami Lakshmanjoo, *Special Verses on Practice*, verse 65, USF archive. For an explanation of *nirvikalpa*, see Appendix A-11.

that *para tattvaṁ*, that supreme state of God consciousness, the supreme state of Parabhairava, *tasmin*, in that (*śivaṁ*), *tasmin sivādi-dharāntaṁ jagat viśvam*[46], *tasmin ṣaṭtriṁśad-ātma*, all of this universe, which is from *pṛthivī* to *śiva tattva*[47], it is existing in that *para tattva*[48].

PS DVD 1 (00:42:07)

दर्पणबिम्बे यद्वन्
नगरग्रामादि चित्रमविभागि ।
भाति विभागेनैव च
परस्परं दर्पणादपि च ॥१२॥
विमलतमपरमभैरव-
बोधात् तद्वद् विभागशून्यमपि
अन्योन्यं च ततोऽपि च
विभक्तमाभाति जगदेतत् ॥१३॥

darpaṇa-bimbe yadvan
nagara-grāmādi citram-avibhāgi /
bhāti vibhāgenaiva ca
paras-paraṁ darpaṇādapi ca //12//
vimalatama-parama-bhairava-
bodhāt tatvad vibhāga-śūnyam-api /
anyonyaṁ ca tato'pi ca
vibhaktam-ābhāti jagad-etat //13//

---

46 शिवतत्वं तस्मिन् शिवादिधरान्तं जगत् विश्वम्
Śivatattvaṁ, tasmin sivādi-dharāntaṁ jagat viśvam. (Swami Lakshmanjoo's handwritten notes)

47 Kashmir Shaivism recognizes 36 elements from *pṛthvī* (earth) to Śiva (the Absolute). See Appendix A-12.

48 "This universe is the manifestation of Bhairava [in *bheda-bhāva*, the differentiated state], and Bhairava is at the same time one with His own nature in *abheda-bhāva*, the undifferentiated state. So, in both ways, there is no difference in His nature." (Swami Lakshmanjoo's handwritten notes)

One *śloka*–in this, there are two *ślokas*–one *śloka* is the example, and the other *śloka* is the actual state of Parabhairava, how the actual state of Parabhairava is existing. And, for this, he gives an example.

Darpaṇa bimbe yadvat. Take an outside mirror, keep the mirror in your room here, *darpaṇa bimbe*, and see–but keep this a well-cleaned mirror–*nagaragrāmādi citram avibhāgi, nagaragrām*, whatever is reflected in it, you see everything is reflected in the mirror, which is only two feet by two feet–two feet length and two feet height, *bas*, only this much–and in this [mirror], you will feel the reflection of this house, the reflection of that house, the reflection of those trees, big trees, the reflection of everything, whatever you . . . it is reflected on this. *Citram* means [that the various reflections are] not put in one ball there [in the mirror], because the dimension of this mirror is only two feet by two feet. [The actual objects that are reflected] can't come in two feet by two feet. It seems separate; *bhāti vibhāgenaiva ca*, and it seems separate.

Nacaya etat dharmanasya prasyato yujyate.[49] You can't [understand even] after investigation what has happened to this, how these trees seem to exist away from the [surface] of the mirror, back [i.e., behind the mirror]. But, after investigating what is in the back, there is nothing, There is nothing. Only distance is seen, distance is observed. And, at the same time, there is also no weight in this [reflection]. For instance, a big tree trunk has [been] reflected in this mirror. If the weight of the mirror was one kilo, after the reflection of this tree of a hundred kilos, it does not create . . .

JONATHAN: Extra weight.

SWAMIJI: . . . extra weight. [The mirror remains] the same weight. [Otherwise] you couldn't move [the mirror]; then you couldn't move it [laughter]. *Dharmaṇo'pi achālasyat*, he has said, Abhinavagupta has said, that *dharmaṇo'pi achālasyat*, you could not move it! In weight also, [the mirror remains] the same weight. It is only one kilo.

So this is the glamour of reflection. [The reflections] are separate from each other and separate from the mirror also–what[ever] is reflected in this. This is an example. Now, the main

---

49 Yogarāja's commentary.

thing which is to be understood:

In the same way,

vimalatama-parama-bhairava-
bodhāt tatvad vibhāga-śūnyam-api / *13a* [repeated]

In the same way, that which is absolutely most pure, the purest element, i.e., Parabhairava[50] (Parabhairava is the purest element of the supreme mirror), and in that supreme mirror, which is the purest element of Bhairava, in that Bhairava, *vibhaktama jagad etat*, [all of] this from Śiva to *pṛthvī* (earth), all of this universe, you perceive that universe absolutely separate from Bhairava, from that mirror, from Parabhairava. It [seems] absolutely separate from Parabhairava. And not only that. It is separate from each other; *pṛthvī* (earth) is separated from *jala* (water), *jala* is separated from *agni* (fire), *agni* is separated from *vayu* (wind), *vayu* is separate, *ākāśa* (ether) is separate, the *antaḥkaraṇas* (mind, intellect, and ego) are separate, *śabda* (sound), *sparśa* (touch), *rūpa* (form), *rasa* (taste), and *gandha* (smell) are separate; *prakṛti*, *pṛthvī*, *jala*, and *māyā*, *śuddhavidyā*, *īśvara*, and *sadāśiva* are all separate. *Vibhaktamābhāti*, in the same way, this whole universe shines in the mirror of Parabhairava.

PS DVD 1 (00:48:20)

शिव-शक्ति-सदाशिवता-
मीश्वर-विद्यामयीं च तत्त्वदशाम् ।
शक्तीनां पञ्चानां
विभक्तभावेन भासयति ॥१४॥

śiva-śakti-sadāśivatām-
īśvara-vidyā-mayīṁ ca tattva-daśām /
śaktīnāṁ pañcānāṁ
vibhakta-bhāvena bhāsayati //*14*//

---

50 "In [an ordinary] mirror, this universe appears from outside the mirror, but in the mirror of Bhairava, this universe appears by His *svātantrya* only." (Swami Lakshmanjoo's handwritten notes)

Now, as you already know, the readers also already know, that there are five great elements: *śiva*, *śakti*, *sadāśiva*, *īśvara* and *śuddhavidyā*. These are the five purest elements of manifestation. This is the first manifestation, pure manifestation, which has begun from *śiva tattva*. *Śiva tattva* and *śakti* [are actually] one element. *Sadāśiva tattva* is the second element, *īśvara tattva* is the third element, and *śuddhavidyā tattva* is the fourth element. And *śakti* is the second element. *Śiva* is the first element, *śakti tattva* is the second element, *sadāśiva tattva* is the third element, *īśvara tattva* is the fourth element, and *śuddhavidyā tattva* is the fifth element.[51] These five pure elements, *śaktīnāṁ pañcānāṁ vibhakta*, these first five pure elements have appeared, have been created; *śaktīnāṁ pañcānāṁ vibhakta bhāvena*, when these five energies have appeared (*vibhakta bhāvena*).

In *śiva tattva*, there is only the manifestation . . . the *yogi* perceives in *śiva tattva* only *śiva tattva*. *Śakti tattva* is one with that. When you perceive the state of *sakti tattva*, in that *śakti tattva*, the first-class *yogi* perceives, in *śakti tattva*, two elements: *śiva tattva* and *śakti tattva*. When he beholds *sadāśiva tattva*, in that *sadāśiva tattva*, the *yogi* perceives . . . how many elements?

DENISE: Three.

SWAMIJI: Three elements, *shabhash*! *Śiva tattva*, *śakti tattva*, and *sadāśiva tattva*. In *īśvara tattva*, [the *yogi* perceives] *śiva tattva*, *śakti tattva*, *sadāśiva tattva*, and *īśvara tattva*. And in *śuddhavidyā*, you hold all the five energies.

---

51 "Śiva has taken five formations of His pure nature of God consciousness. The first formation and the supreme one is *śiva*, and the second is *śakti*, the third is *sadāśiva*, the fourth is *īśvara*, and the fifth is *śuddhavidyā*. *Śiva ādi śuddhavidyāntaṁ*, just right from *śiva* up to *śuddhavidya*, *yat śivasya svakaṁ vapuḥ*, these are the formations of Śiva Himself without any distinction. There is no distinction of *bheda* (duality) there. *Śiva* is filled with God consciousness, *śakti* is filled with God consciousness, *sadāśiva* is filled with God consciousness, *īśvara* is filled with God consciousness, and *śuddhavidya* is filled with God consciousness. God consciousness is already full in these five states. So hence, these five states are Śiva's own states, [His] own pure states." Swami Lakshmanjoo, *Tantrāloka* 6.41, USF archive. For a further explanation of the *śuddha tattvas* (pure elements), see *Kashmir Shaivism–The Secret Supreme*, 1.1-9.

śaktīnāṁ pañcānāṁ
vibhakta-bhāvena bhāsayati //*14*// [repeated]

This is the way of creation, how it appears in this world. And He makes you feel [it] like that [i.e., differentiatedly]. Actually, it is not felt like that. If you go to its "truth-ness", then there is nothing. Nothing is created. Nothing has begun to create. It is all the drama of one Parabhairava and the collection of all of these energies.

PS DVD 1 (00:52:02)

परमं यत् स्वातन्त्र्यं
दुर्घटसंपादनं महेशस्य ।
देवी मायाशक्तिः
स्वात्मावरणं शिवस्यैतत् ॥ १५ ॥

paramaṁ yat svātantryaṁ
durghaṭa-saṁpādanaṁ maheśasya /
devī māyā-śaktiḥ
svātmāvaraṇaṁ śivasyaitat //*15*//

The greatest *svātantrya*[52] of Lord Śiva is *durghaṭa saṁpādanaṁ*, which is not possible [for] any limited being to handle. No one has any power to handle like this. That is *durghaṭa saṁpādanam.*

Durghaṭa saṁpādanam. What is and what is not; what is becomes [what] is not, what is not becomes [what] is, by the *svātantrya* of the *māyā śakti* of Parabhairava. What is, that becomes [what is] not, and what is not, that becomes [what] is.

DENISE: Like what's possible becomes impossible, . . .

SWAMIJI: Yes.

DENISE: . . . and what's impossible becomes possible.

SWAMIJI: Impossible. [That] which is possible, that becomes impossible. [That] which is impossible, that becomes possible

52 Absolute freedom. For an explanation of *svātantrya śakti*, see Appendix A-2.

[laughs]. This is the *svātantrya* of Parabhairava.

It was not possible for Parabhairava to become *jīva* (the limited individual); and [for] *jīva* to become Parabhairava, it is not possible. But *jīva* becomes Parabhairava; Parabhairava becomes *jīva*. This is just *māyā śakti*. This is *māyā śakti*. This is the courses. These are the courses of Parabhairava.

By *māyā śakti*, He makes you get absorbed in the dreaming state [and remain concerned with] what I am dreaming. [For example], I dream that we are no more existing. And I dream, sometimes, we are all existing. [But] existence and non-existence, it has no value.

It is *durghaṭa saṁpādanaṁ maheśasya*. And this is the conduct, the real conduct, of the *māyā śakti* of *svātantrya*, His *svātantrya*.

And that is *svātmāvaraṇaṁ śivasya*, this is the covering by which He covers His own body. Who? Parabhairava. Parabhairava just covers His own body and He is nowhere available in the market. You cannot find [Him] although you go on searching day and night, with no news.

PS DVD 1 (00:55:10)

मायापरिग्रहवशाद्
बोधो मलिनः पुमान् पशुर्भवति ।
काल-कला-नियतिवशाद्
रागाविद्यावशेन संबद्धः ॥ १६ ॥

māyā-parigraha-vaśād
bodho malinaḥ pumān paśur-bhavati /
kāla-kalā-niyati-vaśād
rāgāvidyā-vaśena saṁbaddhaḥ //16//

Bodha means *sarvajñatva sarvakartṛtva māyo'pi'bodhaḥ*. *Bodha*, God, is capable of all-doing (*sarvakartṛtva*), capable of all-knowledge (*sarvajñatva*), all-knowing, but *māyā parigraha vaśād*, He, by His *māyā parigraha,* by *māyā svīkāreṇa*, He asks *māyā* to overwhelm My *bodha*.

DENISE: What does that mean?

SWAMIJI: To subside My *bodha*. I want to have My *bodha* subsided by *māyā*.

DENISE: What is *bodha*? My greatness?

SWAMIJI: My all-knowing energy and all-doing energy, I want to subside it [laughter].

And by inviting that *māyā* to attack Him so that He will not be capable of all-knowing and all-doing, *parigraha vaśāt*, He becomes the slave of *māyā*. *Pāratantrībhūtatvāt*, and He becomes *paśu*, He becomes the individual soul afterwards. *Paśu* means *māyāyāḥ pālyaḥ*. *Māyāyāḥ pālyaḥ pāśyaśc*, *māyā* takes care of His livelihood and *māyā* also binds Him in Her rope so that He won't go ahead and ask for returning again to the Parabhairava state. He is stuck, He is stuck with *māyā*.

Kāla kalā niyati vaśāt. *Kāla*, *kalā*, *niyati*, *rāga*, and *avidyā*, by these He becomes entangled.[53]

Kāla entangles Him so that He will not become eternal, He will not be eternally existing. There is a period [of His existence]. *Kāla* means He is only in the present. In the past, He won't exist. In the future, He won't exist. In the present, He will exist. *Kāla* means [His] eternity is subsided and He becomes limited in the cycle of time. He has become the slave of time.

And He is *kalā*. *Kalā* means [that His] all-doing action has subsided and He has taken the position of *kalā*, only some limited action.

Niyati: He is all-pervading, and, by this limitation, He pervades only in the United States in His own house. He is nowhere [else] found. Otherwise, He was everywhere found.

Rāga: He was *pūrṇa*, He was full, without any wanting, and He is full of wants now; He needs, He needs things. He finds, "There is a gap [in] Me. I want this, I want this, I want this." *Rāga* is wanting for everything. There is wantage. You know wantage?

"Do you want a pot?"

"Yes, I want a pot!"

"Do you want a duster?"

"Yes, I want a duster."

"Do you want gloves?"

---

53 Along with *māyā*, these consititue the *ṣaṭ* (six) *kañcukas* (coverings).

"Yes, I want gloves."
It is . . .

DENISE: Never-ending.

SWAMIJI: No. It is attachment for everything, it is desire for having everything.

Niyati means the desire for having only a particular thing. That is *niyati*. "I want, *bas*, another suit. *Bas*, that is all, because I need another suit." That is *niyati*.[54]

And *avidyā*: *avidyā* means limited knowledge. Unlimited knowledge is finished. Limited knowledge is there.[55]

By this, He is *saṁbaddhaḥ*; *saṁbaddhaḥ* means He has become a limited being.

END Paramārthasara DVD 1 (01:01:17)

---

54 *Niyati* is the covering that attaches you to a particular situation, time, or place. [*Editor's note*]

55 "*Kalā*, *vidyā*, *rāga*, *kāla*, and *niyati*, these five elements are just offsprings of, offshoots of, *māyā*. *Kalā* means the capacity of doing something, *vidyā* means the capacity of knowing something, *rāga* means the capacity of some attachment (not universal attachment), *niyati* means the capacity of limitation of space, *kāla* means the limitation of time." Swami Lakshmanjoo, Tantrāloka 9.41, USF archive. For a further explanation of the *kañcukas*, see Appendix A-4.

DVD Two

Now, [Abhinavagupta] defines, clarifies, what is meant by that. In clear words, he makes it clear.

PS DVD 2 (00:00:10)

अधुनैव किंचिदेवे-
दमेव सर्वात्मनैव जानामि ।
मायासहितं कञ्चुक-
षट्कमणोरन्तरङ्गमिदमुक्तम् ॥१७॥

adhunaiva kiṁcid-eve-
dameva sarvātmanaiva jānāmi /
māyā-sahitaṁ kañcuka-
ṣaṭkam-aṇor-antar-aṅgam-idam-uktam //17//
[not recited]

Adhunaiva, it is the limitation of time (*kāla*). *Adhunaiva*, only in the present, e.g., "I am now in 1989."

JONATHAN: 1990.

SWAMIJI: 1990. "I am in 1990. I [am] not existing in 1981. I am existing only in 1990. [In] 1920, I don't know if I existed or not." [This is] *adhunaiva*.

So, this squeezes Him in time. Although He was timeless–He was in the present, He was in the past, and in the future–He is only residing in the present period.

Kiṁcit eva, He is only alert and a master in computer work, but He won't do any other work; He cannot do that [other work].[56] All mismanagement appears to Him of everything. Completion He has lost altogether and there is only limitation. *Kiṁcit eva*, e.g., "I can do only some job. I can [only do this particular] work."

Idam eva–this is *niyati*–*idam eva* means only, e.g., "I am now

56 This is the limitation of *kalā*, limited action.

undergoing my eighty-third year. The eighty-second year is gone. The eighty-fourth year has not yet come. I am only . . . ." That is the limitation of time.[57]

Sarvātma naiva means, e.g., "I want . . . everything is lacking in me. I want to fulfill myself with things. I want to store [things]."[58]

Jānāmi [means, e.g.], "I know only *Tantrāloka*. I know only Shaivism. I don't know Vedānta. I don't know anything [else]."[59]

Māyā sahitaṁ, along with *māyā*, this is *kañcuka ṣaṭkam*[60], this is the six-fold covering, and it is *antaraṅgam*, it is a very subtle covering.

There are three ways of covering. This is the subtle covering. And another is the gross covering. And the center is . . .

JOHN: Medium?

SWAMIJI: . . . medium. Just as the gross covering is in a seed, that outside cover which is separated from that [medium covering]. That is the gross covering.[61]

JOHN: The seed husk.

SWAMIJI: Seed husk. That [outer] covering, which is called *keser*[62], what you [use] in mudding walls. You mix that in the mudding [for] walls–that *keser*.[63] That is the husk?

JONATHAN: Yes.

SWAMIJI: And another is the medium covering. The medium covering is when you pound it, there is some dust, but it has got some grossness. And another is which you cannot separate [from

---

57 "*Niyati* is that I am living in such-and-such place, in such-and-such time." Swami Lakshmanjoo, *Tantrāloka* 11.37, USF archive.

58 This is the limitation of *rāga*, general, unspecific attachment.

59 This is the limitation of *vidyā*, limited knowledge.

60 This is called *māyāṇḍa*, the egg-shaped circle of *māyā*, where the elements from *māyā* to *puruṣa* reside. Six *kañcukas* are including *puruṣa*. "*Puruṣa* means 'covered being'." Swami Lakshmanjoo, *Tantrāloka* 10.99-100, USF archive.

61 Here, the subtle, medium, and gross coverings refer to the egg-shaped circles of *māyā aṇḍa*, *prakṛti aṇḍa*, and *pṛthvī aṇḍa*, as previously mentioned in verse 4. See also Appendix A-8.

62 Rice husk.

63 The outer husk of rice (*keser*) is mixed with earth and used as mud plaster on walls.

the kernel]. That is the internal covering (*antaraṅga*). That is this kind of [subtle] *kañcuka*[64].

Antaraṅga kañcuka, and the medium *kañcuka* (the medium covering), and the gross covering.

PS DVD 2 (00:05:19)

कम्बुकमिव तण्डुलकण-
विनिविष्टं भिन्नमप्यभिदा ।
भजते तत्तु विशुद्धिं
शिवमार्गौन्मुख्ययोगेन ॥१८॥

kambukam-iva taṇḍula-kaṇa-
viniviṣṭaṁ bhinnam-apyabhidā /
bhajate tat-tu viśuddhiṁ
śiva-mārgaunmukhya-yogena //18//

It is the eighteenth *śloka*.

Kambukamiva, just like *kambuk* (*kambuk* means *komb*; *komb* means that husk), although it is *taṇḍulakaṇa viniviṣṭaṁ*, it is just fast-attached with the rice, *bhinnam api*, although it is separate . . .

Because it has vitamins; it can only be separated by pounding it. And it will be a very fine dust. Fine dust, that is that yeast, like that yeast. You know yeast?

. . . although it is separated–but it is just like yeast; that is the internal covering–*bhajate tattu viśuddhiṁ*, and that is clarified, that is removed, that is only removed–but not by effort–that is only removed by the *śaktipāta* (grace), the *śaktipāta* of Parabhairava. If there is *tīvra śaktipāta* of Parabhairava, that internal covering is removed. Otherwise, there is no hope of its removal. It needs *śaktipāta*[65], the will of Lord Śiva.

Now, this [was] the covering of *māyā*. Now, the covering of *prakṛti*. *Prakṛti* is the medium way of covering.[66]

64 Here, *kañcuka* is being used in the literal sense as "covering".

65 For the nine levels of *śaktipāta*, see Appendix A-7.

66 *Prakṛti aṇḍa*, the egg-shaped circle of *prakṛti*, consists of the elements from *jala* (water) to *prakṛti*.

PS DVD 2 (00:07:51)

सुख-दुःख-मोहमात्रं
निश्चय-संकल्पनाभिमानाच्च ।
प्रकृतिरथान्तःकरणं
बुद्धि-मनोऽहङ्कृतिःक्रमशः ॥१९॥

sukha-duḥkha-moha-mātraṁ
niścaya-saṁkalpanābhimānāc-ca /
prakṛtir-athāntaḥ-karaṇaṁ
buddhi-mano'haṅkṛtiḥ-kramaśa / / 19 / /

Prādhānika, etadevā bhogyaṁ bhavati.[67] *Prādhānika sarga* is the creation of covering by *prakṛti*. That [previous one] was the creation of covering by *māyā*, that subtlest [covering]. This is the creation of covering by *prakṛti*.

Sukha means *sattoguṇa*, *duḥkha* means *rajoguṇa*, and *mohamātraṁ* is *tamoguṇa*–these three *guṇas*.[68] And *niścaya* means the intellect, *saṁkalpana* is the mind, and *abhimānāḥ ca* is the ego. *Prakṛtir*, and *prakṛti*. It is *prakṛti*, *antaḥkaraṇaṁ*[69], *kramaśa* (respectively).

How many are they?

First is *prakṛti*, and *āntahkaraṇa* is three (*mana*, *ahaṁkara*, and *buddhi*), and *sāttvaguṇa*, *rājoguṇa*, and *tāmoguṇa*. *Sāttvaguṇa*, *rājoguṇa*, and *tāmoguṇa* are three, and *mana* (mind), *buddhi* (intellect), and *ahaṁkara* (ego), and *prakṛti*.

How many?

JOHN: Seven.

---

67 *Prādhānika, etadevā bhogyaṁ bhavati*: "As there must be an object for this limited subject who is the enjoyer, (the author) explains those *tattvas* which are within *prakṛti*." *Paramārthasāra*, with Yogarājas commentary, translated by John Hughes, Ishwar Ashram, Srinagar Kashmir. (PhD thesis, McMaster University, Hamilton, Ontario, 1972.) See Appendix B also for additional translation of verses.

68 For *prakṛti* and the three *guṇas*, see Appendix A-1.

69 The internal organs.

SWAMIJI: And the eighth is the *puruṣa*[70], who is entangled. They [i.e., the previous seven] entangle Him.

PS DVD 2 (00:10:01)

श्रोत्रं त्वगक्षि रसना
घ्राणं बुद्धीन्द्रियाणि, शब्दादौ ।
वाक्पाणि-पाद-पायू-
पस्थं कर्मेन्द्रियाणि पुनः ॥२०॥

śrotraṁ tvag-akṣi rasanā
ghrāṇaṁ buddhīndriyāṇi, śabdādau /
vāk-pāṇi-pāda-pāyū-
pasthaṁ karmendriyāṇi punaḥ //20//

Śrotraṁ–now, these are now gross–*śrotraṁ* [means] . . .

JOHN: Hearing.

SWAMIJI: . . . ear, *tvak* (touch), *akṣi* (*akṣi* means *netra*[71]), . . .

Akṣi has got two ways: one *akṣi* is the internal process by which there is a connection with *ahaṁkāra* (the ego). And [the second] *akṣi* is only *golaka*. It has nothing to do with *ahaṁkāra*[72]. *Akṣi* is *golaka*, that [physical] eye. When the eye is open and the mind is not working, you can't see with the eye. When the mind is there, that *akṣi* is with *ahaṁkāra*. It has nothing to do with *ahaṁkara*, i.e., this [physical] eye. This is just with the body. At the time of death, this eye cannot–although it is open–it cannot observe anything, it cannot see anything. And, in the same way, *ghrāṇāṁ* (these *buddhīndriyāṇi*, *jñānendriyāṇi*[73]), and *śabdā-*

---

70 The limited sentient being or soul. "He is really Lord Śiva, always." Swami Lakshmanjoo, *Tantrāloka* 9.155, USF archive.

71 Sight.

72 The ego.

73 *Buddhīndriyāṇi* and *jñānendriyāṇi* are synonymous terms meaning the organs of cognition or knowledge, which are comprised of *śrotraṁ* (ear), *tvak* (skin), *cakṣu* (eye), *rasanā* (tongue), and *ghrāṇā* (nose). See Introduction and also *Kashmir Shaivism–The Secret Supreme*, 1.2-6.

dau[74], [and] *vāk, pāṇi, pāda, pāyu, upastha* (the *karmendriyāṇi*[75]), these also vanish at the time of death.[76]

The twentieth [*śloka*] is finished.

PS DVD 2 (00:12:23)

एषां ग्राह्यो विषयः
सूक्ष्मः प्रविभागवर्जितो यः स्यात् ।
तन्मात्रपञ्चकं तत्
शब्दः स्पर्शो महो रसो गन्धः ॥२१॥

eṣāṁ grāhyo viṣayaḥ
sūkṣmaḥ pravibhāga-varjito yaḥ syāt /
tanmātra-pañcakaṁ tat
śabdaḥ sparśo maho raso gandhaḥ //21//

---

74 "That subtle objective field which would be without objective qualification, that is the pentad of the *tanmātrās* which are (*śabda*) sound, (*sparśa*) touch sensation, (*rūpa maha* or *maharūpa*?) form, (*rasa*) flavor, (*gandhaḥ*) smell." *Paramārthasāra*, with Yogarājas commentary, translated by John Hughes, Ishwar Ashram, Srinagar Kashmir. (PhD thesis, McMaster University, Hamilton, Ontario, 1972.) See also *Kashmir Shaivism–The Secret Supreme*, 1.4.

75 The five organs of action are *vāk* (speech), *pāṇi* (hand), *pāda* (foot), *pāyu* (organ of excretion), *upastha* (creative organ). See *Kashmir Shaivism–The Secret Supreme*, 1.2-4.

76 "*Puryaṣṭaka* carries the impressions again and again [from birth to birth], extracts impressions. Otherwise, if *puryaṣṭaka* is not existing, at the time of death you'll be united with God automatically, without doing anything. *Puryaṣṭaka* is the trouble-maker." Swami Lakshmanjoo, *Parātrīśikā Vivaraṇa*, USF archive.

"When the five *tanmātras* give rise to the three intellectual organs (intellect, mind, and ego), then collectively there are eight organs. These eight organs are said to be *puryaṣṭaka* [lit. the "city of eight"] and they function in our dreaming state. This *puryaṣṭaka* prevents you from getting through to the reality of your Self. When the reality of your nature is ignored, then you are dependent on enjoyment which cannot be refused. Because of this you are played and entangled by the wheel of repeated birth and deaths." Swami Lakshmanjoo's translation of *Spanda Karikā* 3.17-18 from *Śiva Sūtra–The Supreme Awakening*, 3.2 commentary.

These [*tanmātras* are] *śabda*, *sparśa*, *rūpa*, *rasa*, and *gandha*. *Śabda* (sound) comes out from *śrotra* (the ear), *sparśa* (touch) comes from skin (*tvak*), [*rūpa* (form) comes out from the eyes (*cakṣu*)], [*rasa* (taste)] comes from [*rasana* (the tongue), and *gandha* (smell)] comes from [*ghrāṇā* (the nose)]. These are . . . that smell, etc., [come out from the] *jñānendriyaṇi*[77].

And, in the same way, *śabda*, *sparśa*, *rūpa*, *rasa*, and *gandha* are gross; *śrotra*, *tvak*, *akṣi*, *rasanā*, and *ghrāṇa* are subtle.

PS DVD 2 (00:13:44)

एतत्संसर्गवशात्
स्थूलो विषयस्तु भूतपञ्चकताम् ।
अभ्येति नभः पवन-
स्तेजः सलिलं च पृथ्वी च ॥२२॥

etat-saṁsarga-vaśāt
sthūlo viṣayastu bhūta-pañcakatām /
abhyeti nabhaḥ pavanas-
tejaḥ salilaṁ ca pṛthvī ca //22//

When it goes another step, more outside, then there is the gross *viṣaya*[78], and the gross field of this creation becomes the *pañca mahābhūta*: *pṛthvī* (earth), *jala* (water), *agni* (fire), *vayu* (air), and *ākāśa* (space, ether)–these five great elements. They are absolutely gross. [The five *tanmātras*] become the five *bhūtas* (great elements).[79]

PS DVD 2 (00:14:43)

तुष इव तण्डुलकणिका-
मावृणुते प्रकृतिपूर्वकः सर्गः ।

77 The organs of knowledge. See *Kashmir Shaivism–The Secret Supreme*, 1.2-5.

78 Sphere.

79 See *Tantrāloka* 9 for a detailed discussion of the genesis of the elements.

पृथ्वीपर्यन्तोऽयं
चैतन्यं देहभावेन ॥२३॥

tuṣa iva taṇḍula-kaṇikām-
āvṛṇute prakṛti-pūrvakaḥ sargaḥ /
pṛthvī-paryanto'yaṁ
caitanyaṁ deha-bhāvena //23//

Tuṣa iva taṇḍula-kaṇikām-āvṛṇute. Just like *dhānya carma* (*dhānya carma* means that gross [covering])–he goes again to that first step, that gross covering of a seed–which *taṇḍula kaṇikāma āvṛṇute*, that grain of rice is covered by that gross covering, that is equal to *prakṛti pūrvakaḥ sargaḥ*. This is the creation from *prakṛti* [to] *pṛthvī paryanta* (up to *pṛthvī*). And it covers *caitanyaṁ*, the consciousness residing in the body, by pushing consciousness in the bodily being. He then realizes, "I am living". He nominates ["I"] to His body, not to that internal blissful state of consciousness.

[Introduction to verse 24]

So, in other words, [the coverings are] *parā*, *sūkṣma*, and *sthūla*; gross (*sthūla*), subtle (*parā*), and medium (*sūkṣma*), these three *malas*[80], which cover this Parabhairava state, by His own free will.

PS DVD 2 (00:16:56)

परमावरणं मल इह,
सूक्ष्मं मायादि कञ्चुकं, स्थूलम् ।
बाह्यं विग्रहरूपं,
कोशत्रयवेष्टितो ह्यात्मा ॥२४॥

80 Although the literal meaning of *mala* is "impurity", as in the verse quoted above from the invocation of the *Bhojavṛtti*, Bhoja's commentary on Patañjali's *Yoga Sūtras* (see commentary on verses 2 and 3), according to Kashmir Shaivism, "the *malas* are just the absence of knowledge, and not something substantial." Swami Lakshmanjoo, *Tantrāloka* 9.75, USF archives.

paramāvaraṇaṁ mala iha,
sūkṣmaṁ māyādi kañcukaṁ, sthūlam /
bāhyaṁ vigraha-rūpaṁ,
kośa-traya-veṣṭito hyātmā //24//

By these three coverings, Śiva, in the formation of being an individual, is enwrapped. I have written its meaning on one side.[81] *Āṇavamala* is supreme, and [less] subtle is *māyīyamala*, and gross is *kārmamala*.

Kārmamala, by which he says, "I am fine, I am *sukhi* (I am happy), I am not happy, I am painful", like that. That is *kārmamala*, by action.

Kośa traya veṣṭito hyātmā, these three coverings cover this God consciousness totally, so that It cannot be freed from this covering. [He is] stuck in *māyā* by His own free will.

JOHN: Those three *malas*, they correspond to those three: subtle, gross, and medium.

SWAMIJI: Yes.

JOHN: So gross is *kārmamala*, . . .

SWAMIJI: Yes.

JOHN: . . . and medium is *māyīyamala*, and subtle is *āṇavamala*.

SWAMIJI: *Āṇavamala*, yes.[82]

PS DVD 2 (00:18:44)

अज्ञान-तिमिरयोगाद्
एकमपि स्वं स्वभावमात्मानम् ।
ग्राह्य-ग्राहकनाना-
वैचित्र्येणावबुध्येत ॥२५॥

81 परंमलं = आणवं, सूक्ष्मंमलं = मायीयम् , स्थूलंमलं = कार्ममलं – *paraṁ malaṁ = āṇavam, sūkṣmaṁ malam = māyīyam, sthūlaṁ malam = kārmamalam.* "By these three coverings, Śiva, in the formation of being an individual, is enwrapped." (Swami Lakshmanjoo's handwritten notes)

82 For a further explanation of the *malas*, see Appendix A-3 and also *Kashmir Shaivism–The Secret Supreme*, 7.47-49.

ajñāna-timira-yogād
ekam-api svaṁ svabhāvam-ātmānam /
grāhya-grāhaka-nānā-
vaicitryeṇāvabudhyeta //25//

Ajñāna timira yogāt, it is a kind of [disease]; He accepts this kind of disease in His own nature. In His divine nature, He accepts [this] disease, He invites this disease of seeing many through the pupil of His eye. It is a kind of disease by which you see a gang of moons; when you look at the moon, you will see a gang of moons with this eye. This is your own defect in your eyes. This is a disease. He invites that disease by His play. [The disease is] *ajñāna* (ignorance).

Ajñāna timira (*timira* means *katsha timira*), *timira* is that *katsha timira*[83] by which you cannot see only two moons in one; you see a line of moons, a line of suns, a line of stars. And you ask other people also, "See, there are so many moons!" They are stuck, they are astonished. They say, "No, there is only one moon. What do you [speak]?" [You say], "*Bakwas*[84]! It is *bakwas*! I see it."

So, *grāhya grāhakanānā vaicitryeṇa*, and He sees [that] there is Jonathan, there is John Hughes, there is Viresh, there is Denise, there is Lakshmanjoo, there is Bhagawan Das, there are so many individuals. Although there is one Being, one Parabhairava, one Parabhairava has become many and He realizes many in one.

So, it is a kind of disease [that] He has invited for Him[self] by His own play.

grāhyagrāhakanānā-
vaicitryeṇāvabudhyeta //25// [repeated]

He accepts it. He invites it. But, although He invites it and He has become, the One has become, many (*kālakalāni jivaśat*, He has become one hundred, thousands; the One has become millions), it is His play.

---

83 The literal meaning of *katsha timira,* is to see the moon defectively.
84 Nonsense.

You can't deny it. He sees! Whatever is seen, you cannot say, "No, it is not [there]!" The population is one thousand here. Will you deny it, this population in Nepal? So many disgusted brutes, small brutes; good ones also and poor ones also. There are so many. You cannot deny it.

And so one Being has become many. And this is the play.

PS DVD 2 (00:22:37)

रस-फाणित-शर्करिका-
गुड-खण्डाद्या यथेक्षुरस एव ।
तद्वद् अवस्थाभेदाः
सर्वे परमात्मनः शंभोः ॥२६॥

rasa-phāṇita-śarkarikā-
guḍa-khaṇaḍādyā yatheksu-rasa eva /
tadvad avasthābhedāḥ
sarve paramātmanaḥ śaṁbhoḥ //26//
[verse not recited or translated][85]

Some great soul, Śaṁbhu Bhaṭṭāraka, has said . . .

This Yogarāja, the commentator of this Abhinavagupta's *Paramārthasāra*, he refers to this *śloka* of Śaṁbhu Bhaṭṭāraka. [Śaṁbhu Bhaṭṭāraka] was a great soul.

[He said]:

एको भावः सर्वभावस्वभावः
सर्वे भावा एकभावस्वभावाः ।
एको भावस्तत्त्वतो येन दृष्टः
सर्वे भावास्तत्त्वतस्तेन दृष्टाः ॥

85 "Just as syrup, brown sugar, molasses, and purified sugar are just the juice of the sugar cane, so all these different conditions are Śambhu, the supreme Self." *Paramārthasāra*, John Hughes, 1972.

eko bhāvaḥ sarva-bhāva-svabhāvaḥ
sarve bhāvā ekabhāva-svabhāvāḥ /
eko bhāvas-tattvato yena dṛṣṭaḥ
sarve bhāvās-tattvatastena dṛṣṭāḥ / /

Eko bhāvaḥ, one Being (one Being, that is Śiva, Lord Śiva, Parabhairava) has become *sarva bhāva svabhāva*, He has become many; many, right from that insect to *śānta kala*.[86] He has become so many. *Sarve bhāvā eka bhāva svabhāvā*, and all these are actually *eka bhāva svabhāvā*, actually this is only the drama of One, i.e., Parabhairava, *bas*. It is only *eka bhāva* (one Being). All are one. One are many; The One has become many.

Eko bhāvas-tattvato yena dṛṣṭa, and that fortunate one who has realized what is *eko bhāva* (one Being), who has realized [this] by the *tīvra śaktipāta*[87] of Parabhairava, *sarve bhāvāḥ tattvatastena dṛṣṭā*, he has realized all beings.

So, all beings are equal to one Being, one Being is equal to all beings. There is no difference between all beings and one Being.

Right?

Bhagavadgītāsvapi, in the *Bhagavad Gītā* also, Lord Kṛṣṇa explains this to Arjuna:

सर्वभूतेषु येनैकं भावमक्षयमीक्षते ।
अविभक्तं विभक्तेषु तज्ज्ञानं विद्धि सात्त्विकम् ॥

sarva-bhūteṣu yenaikaṁ bhāvamakṣayamīkṣate /
avibhaktaṁ vibhakteṣu tajjñānaṁ viddhi sāttvikam / /[88]

Śāttvic knowledge is that, by which knowledge, by which *sāttvic* knowledge, a fortunate person sees only one *bhāva*, one

---

86 "When the agitation and tides of these six-fold coverings are over (*kañcuka taraṅga upaśamāt*), *śāntā nāma kalā*, that is called *śāntā kalā*. *Śāntā kalā* is that circle in which circle all agitations of these six-fold coverings are over. This *śāntā kalā* exists, *sā ca śuddhavidyādiśaktyante sthitā iti*, from *śuddhavidyā* element to *śakti*." Swami Lakshmanjoo, *Janma Maraṇa Vicāra*, USF archive. See also Appendix A-8.

87. For *śaktipāta* (grace), see Appendix A-7.

88 *Bhagavad Gītā*, 18.20.

state of being, which is undifferentiated in differentiated; which is undifferentiated . . .

Who is undifferentiated? Bhairava, Being.

. . . in the differentiated world. *Tat jñānaṁ*, that knowledge, is *sāttvic* knowledge, that is the true knowledge. Other [knowledge] of *rājas* and *tāmas* are *bakwas* (nonsense).[89]

PS DVD 2 (00:26:26)

विज्ञानान्तर्यामि-
प्राण-विराड्देह-जाति-पिण्डान्ताः ।
व्यवहारमात्रमेतत्
परमार्थेन तु न सन्त्येव ॥२७॥

vijñānāntaryāmi-
prāṇa-virāḍ-deha-jāti-piṇḍāntāḥ /
vyavahāra-mātram-etat
paramārthena tu na santyeva //27//

Now, he [mentions] the varieties of, difference of, all philosophers; many, various philosophers, other than Shaivite philosophers.

Some say, "*Vijñāna*, only knowledge, is God."

Some say, "*Antaryāmi*[90] is God."

Some say, "Only breath (*prāṇa*) is God."

Some say, "Universality[91] is God."

Jāti means . . . [some say], "*Jāti*[92], being, is God".

Piṇḍā means, "The body is God". That is *piṇḍā*. That is one

89 "You must understand, you'll know, that *avyayam bhāvam*, that unperishable state of God consciousness is residing in each and every being. . . . In that way, you won't hate anybody. If you hate anybody, it means you don't find the state of God consciousness in that person. If you ever found that the state of God consciousness is in that person, you'd never hate him." Swami Lakshmanjoo, *Bhagavad Gītā* audio, USF archive.

90 *Antaryāmi*, generally translated as "the indwelling soul".

91 The material universe.

92 *Jāti* means "sameness in differentiation". [*Editor's note*]

way of the atheist. They say [that] the body is everything.

Vyavahāra mātram etat, these are just varieties of thoughts, various thoughts. *Paramārthena tu na santyeva*, in fact, in the real sense, from the real point of view, these things do not exist at all. It is only one play of God.

JOHN: What was the second one, sir? The second idea of who was God?

SWAMIJI: *Vijñānaṁ brahma*[93], some say (the *Vijñānavadins*), they calculate, that only knowledge is Brahma. Some say breath is Brahma. Some say universality is Brahma; this universal being, the universe, is Brahma. Some say *jāti* is Brahma.

> *Jāti* means, for instance, as Lord Kriṣṇa has related to Arjuna in the *Bhagavad Gītā*, that, "In trees, I am *aśvattha*"[94]. *Jāti* means, for instance, there are trees, *jāti* means a plum tree. "Plum tree" is differentiated knowledge, "tree" is undifferentiated knowledge. In trees, there is undifferentiated and differentiated knowledge. When you perceive a plum tree, you separate a plum tree from all other trees. That is *jāti*[95].

JOHN: There are undifferentiated and differentiated when we separate? You said that when you see a plum tree, there is differentiated and undifferentiated.

JONATHAN: No, when you see a tree, it is undifferentiated.

SWAMIJI: "Trees" is undifferentiated. In trees, when you utter

---

93 Swamiji is referring to the Brahman, the Absolute, rather than Brahma, the god of creation.

94 "The *aśvattha* tree is existing here in this universe. It has got *urdhva mūlam*, it has got roots in Parabhairava state, in *śantātītākalā*. *Adhaḥ śākham*, the branches of this tree are spread down below in the *kalagnirūdra* down below. And this *aśvattha* [fig tree] is *prāhur*, said to be *avyayam* (imperishable). . . . *Samsāra* is this manifestation of Parabhairava. You have to cut the branches of this *samsāra,* down below, and keep only roots above. Branches are varieties of its manifestation down below in the world." Swami Lakshmanjoo, *Bhagavad Gītā* video, USF archive.

95 The literal meaning of *jāti* is caste, class, breed, or species. [*Editor's note*]

"trees", in trees, all the trees [are included], e.g., a plum tree, a kobhani tree, etc.

JOHN: It is just tree-ness, just tree.

SWAMIJI: Tree. And when you say "plum tree", a plum tree is the differentiated class; "plum tree", that is also differentiated. And when you say "tree", "tree" is the most undifferentiated class. In "tree", all [trees] are woven–in that "tree" word. In "plum tree", only plum trees are woven. In fruit trees . . . it is like that.

JOHN: So which is God in that? God is the undifferentiated totality of everything?

SWAMIJI: The totality . . . [He is] undifferentiated in differentiated beings. Both are appearing side-by-side in this world.

But *vyavahāra mātram etat*, it is just *vyavahāra*.[96] In fact, they are not existing at all, i.e., this undifferentiated and differentiated. It is one play of Lord Śiva.

तीर्थक्रियाव्यसनिनः स्वमनीषिकाभि-
रुत्प्रेक्ष्य तत्त्वमिति यद्यद् अमी वदन्ति ।
तत् तत्त्वमेव भवतोऽस्ति न किंचिदन्यत्
संज्ञासु केवलमयं विदुषां विवादः

tīrtha-kriyāvyasaninaḥ svamanīṣikābhir-
utprekṣya tattvam-iti yadyad amī vadanti /
tat tattvam-eva bhavato'sti na kiṁcidanyat
saṁjñāsu kevalamayaṁ viduṣāṁ vivādaḥ //
[verse from Yogarāja's commentary]

Tīrtha kriyāvyasaninaḥ, those who go deep in the depth of all *śāstras* (*tīrtha* means *śāstras*) and *svamanīṣikābhir utprekṣya*, by their own understanding, *utprekṣya*, they calculate that, "This is the reality of God", they are not on the right path, they are not actually understanding what is the right path. They only think

96 "Worldly activities which reside in differentiatedness, differentiated knowledge." Swami Lakshmanjoo, *Tantrāloka* 7.30, USF archive.

from their limited viewpoint that this is the right path.

Tat tattvameva bhavato'sti na kiṁcidanyat, there are some great souls who know exactly . . . [97]

PS DVD 2 (00:33:03)

रज्ज्वां नास्ति भुजङ्ग-
स्त्रासं कुरुते च मृत्युपर्यन्तम् ।
भ्रान्तेर्महती शक्ति-
र्न विवेक्तुं शक्यते नाम ॥२८॥

rajjvāṁ nāsti bhujaṅgas-
trāsaṁ kurute ca mṛtyu-paryantam /
bhrānter-mahatī śaktir-
na vivektuṁ śakyate nāma //28//
[not recited in full]

asadarthapratipādanasāmarthyam[98]
[comm. introduction to verse 28]

That which is not existing, and, with your misunderstanding, you make it existent by your misunderstanding. You don't understand it properly, in the right way, and you misunderstand it, and you make it appear that way.

DENISE: You make yourself believe its real but its not.

JOHN: Which number?

SWAMIJI: Twenty-eight.

Rajjvāṁ nāsti bhujaṅgas. Rajjvāṁ, in that perception of a rope, *nāsti bhujaṅga*, the existence of perceiving a snake is not

---

97 "Whatever these people busy themselves with the making of philosophy say to reality conceiving it with their minds, that is your reality and nothing else. This disagreement of the philosophers exists only as a matter of words." *Paramārthasāra*, John Hughes, (1972).

98 "Now to establish the unreal, he illustrates the power of illusion." Ibid.

Note: The original text reads "*sāmarthyena*", which Swamiji changes to "*sāmarthyam*". [*Editor's note*]

existing–this existence of perceiving a snake is not there–but, even then, if it is not there, *trāsaṁ kurute ca mṛtyu paryantam*, it creates fear; it creates so much threat that there remains not the slightest . . . nothing is left up to the death, i.e., you die.

DENISE: You die of fright?

SWAMIJI: With fright.

There is an Idgah[99] where, in Srinagar, they perform *namaz* (prayers)–the Mohammedans. That [place is called] Idgah. They perform *namaz* on Fridays, on each Friday. Otherwise, that [Idgah] is so great, it is so big, it is more than one hundred times bigger than the ground of the [palace of the] king of Nepal–that ground.

DENISE: It is a huge area.

SWAMIJI: Huge area! It is for performing *namaz*. And from all sides of the valley, from villages people come on Fridays and perform *namaz* there. They think that it will be accepted by God, *kudhatāra*, if it is done collectively. And for the remaining period, these days that remain [between each occasion], just there is nobody [occupying that place].
And one person bet with somebody, "I will threaten [i.e., dare] one classmate of mine". And he told him, "If you go at night there . . ."
In that [Idgah], there is a mosque also–in the center, there is a mosque also–and in the mosque, there is an arrangement for washing the feet and everything, and the organs, before performing *namaz*.
. . . he said, "If you go there and [take] this one peg, you stick it [in the ground] before that mosque, then we will give you one hundred rupees when it is there". And he stuck it [in the ground before the mosque]. [But] because it was too dark–it was a dark night and he went there and he had a *pherin*[100]–unfortunately one piece of his *pherin* remained under that peg. And he stuck that peg in the ground, and, when [he tried to come] out, he couldn't. He thought, "I am finished!"

DENISE: Someone had caught him and he died.

---

99 A large ground for offering Ramzan prayers.

100 A traditional loose-fitting Kashmiri robe.

SWAMIJI: And he died of threat.

DENISE: Did this happen recently?

SWAMIJI: Yes, it has happened recently.

DENISE: He died of fright.

SWAMIJI: He died of fright. He was finished. He thought that, "Some ghost has caught me".

This is *bhrānti*. This has got great power. *Trāsaṁ*, it produces that threat up to [the point of causing] death. You cannot explain how great a power it has, i.e., this misunderstanding.

In the same way . . . this was an example. He gives that [explanation] now for which he had given an example:

PS DVD 2 (00:39:22)

तद्वद् धर्माधर्म-
स्वर्निरयोत्पत्ति-मरण-सुख-दुःखम् ।
वर्णाश्रमादि चात्म-
न्यसदपि विभ्रमबलाद्भवति ॥२९॥

tadvad dharmādharma-
svar-nirayotpatti-maraṇa-sukha-duḥkham /
varṇāśramādi cātmany-
asadapi vibhrama-balād-bhavati //29//

Vibhrama balād–tadvad, in the same way–*vibhrama balād*, when *māyā* is in force, [when] *māyā* is handling with its force to individuals, although good actions (*dharma*), *ādharma* (bad actions), *svar* means heaven, *niraya* means hell, *utpatti* means birth, *maraṇa* means death, *sukha* means pleasure, *duḥkha* means pain, *varṇāśramādi* (e.g., "I am a *brahmin*, I am a *kṣatriya*, I am a *vaiśya*", etc.), . . .

This kind of perceiving that, "I am a *brahmin* with good qualifications. I am the topmost head of these *aśramās*. I am a *brahmin*. I have got *tilak*." [That is] *varṇa*.[101] [This] is *āśrama*[102]: "I am

101 Caste (*varṇa*) consciousness.

brahmacāri[103], I am *gṛhastha* (householder), I am *vānaprasta* (forest-dweller), and I am a *sanyāsī* (renunciate)." That is *āśramā*[104].

. . . *atmani asad api*, [although] it is not existing in the state of Parabhairava, *vibhrama balād*, but, by misunderstanding, it appears and it works like that.

Another *śloka*:

PS DVD 2 (00:41:07)

एतत् तद् अन्धकारं
यद् भावेषु प्रकाशमानतया ।
आत्मानतिरिक्तेष्वपि
भवत्यनात्माभिमानोऽयम् ॥३०॥

etat tad andhakāraṁ
yad bhāveṣu prakāśa-mānatayā /
ātmānatiriktesvapi
bhavaty-anātmābhimāno'yam //30//

---

102 The four stages (*āśrama*) of life.

103 "*Brahmacāri vrata* is not the type of being a bachelor always. *Brahmacārī vrata*, from the Śaiva point of view, is that you should see, you should observe in your mind, that death, life, success, fail, pain, pleasure, sadness, sorrow, happiness, joy, rise, fall, all these are the expansion of His glory. That is *brahmacāri vrata*.

"*Brahmacāri vrata* is [to perceive that] everywhere Brahman is moving, [everywhere] is the movement of God consciousness. Death is the movement of God consciousness, life is the movement of God consciousness. So there is no fear, because the soul is always living, the soul will never die. The body is already dead." Swami Lakshmanjoo, *Bhagavad Gītā* audio, USF archive.

"*Brahmacārī* is the one who experiences this *kuṇḍalinī*. He is *brahmacārī*." Swami Lakshmanjoo, Secret Supreme, USF archive.

104 "*Brahmacāri* is bondage, *gṛhastha* is bondage, *vānaprasta* is bondage, *śuddhavidyā* is bondage, *īśvara* is bondage, *sadāśiva* is bondage. Up to Śiva, everything is bondage." Swami Lakshmanjoo, *Tantrāloka* 8.291, USF archive.

eṣā sā pūrṇat-vākhyāti-rupā-viśva mohinī bhrāntiḥ[105]

Etat tad andhakāraṁ, this is *andhakāra. Andhakāra* is just the darkness of *māyā*, the dark understanding of *māyā*. This is that dark understanding of *māyā*.

What is that?

Yad bhāveṣu prakāśa mānatayā ātmānatirikteṣu, although this whole universe, the objective world of this existing universe, *ātmānatirikteṣu api*, although all of these objective classes of the world are not separated from Bhairava's state, but one feels by *māyā*, by the force of *māyā*, one feels they are separated–although they are not separated.

PS DVD 2 (00:42:36)

तिमिरादपि तिमिरमिदं
गण्डस्योपरि महानयं स्फोटः ।
यदनात्मन्यपि देह-
प्राणादावात्ममानित्वम् ॥ ३१ ॥

timirād-api timiram-idaṁ
gaṇḍasyopari mahānayaṁ sphoṭaḥ /
yad-anātmany-api deha-
prāṇādāvātma-mānitvam //31//

Timirād api timiram idaṁ. It is *timir. Timir* is one disease when you see many in the vision of the eyes. It is more than that. It is [not only] in the eyes [that] you see many, [but also] you smell many, you touch many, you have got many in all of the five senses. Many-ness is beheld by all the senses, not only in vision.

Gaṇḍasyopari mahānayaṁ sphoṭaḥ, it is just like a big boil [that] appears on your cheek, which is already [like] a boil–this cheek is [like a] boil. This is the elevated portion of your [face],

105 "This very (*eṣā sā*) misunderstanding (*bhrāntiḥ*), which deludes the whole world (*viśva-mohinī*), is of the nature of (*rupā*) non-perception/ignorance (*akhyāti-*) of [one's own] Fullness (*pūrṇatva*)." (Swamiji's handwritten note of a paraphrase of Yogarāja's commentary) [*Editor's note*]

this cheek, and on that cheek, when there is a boil, you become [Swamiji demonstrates]. At that time, [your cheek becomes very swollen].

JOHN: So you have a pimple on top of your boil.

SWAMIJI: Yes.

VIRESH: Is that possible?

DENISE: Yeah.

SWAMIJI: It is possible, yes, if there is a boil . . . unluckily, if a boil appears here [on your cheek].

DENISE: It becomes a double boil.

SWAMIJI: You [may] have a boil appear on these fingers and sometime a boil may appear [on the cheek] also, and you look fearful at that moment (*gaṇḍasyopari mahānayaṁ sphoṭaḥ*).

What is that?

Yadanātmani api deha prāṇādāu, although *deha*, *prāṇa*, *puryaṣṭaka*, *śūnya*, all of these differentiated bodies [of the limited individual] . . .

Deha means the body existing in wakefulness, and [*puryaṣṭaka* means] the body existing in the dreaming state, and [*prāṇa* means] the body existing in the dreamless state, and [*śūnya* means] the body existing in the *śūnya* (void) state, where [you experience] nothingness.

. . . in these [fourfold] bodies, you think that, "I am this". Although this is not *ātma*, but he perceives this is *ātma*. This is [like] that kind of disease on your cheek.

JOHN: You think that you are your body.

SWAMIJI: You think that it is your own body.

And Yogarāja, the commentator of this *Paramārthasāra* of Abhinavagupta, puts the reference of Madālasa *yoginī*. She was one female saint, and she was a householder. She had a husband and she had produced children, small children (many, four or five), and she used to insert the knowledge of Parabhairava in the children while feeding them. While they were growing bigger and bigger day-by-day, she would insert supreme knowledge in them. And [the following] *śloka* he has penned down, this Yogarāja. Because Yogarāja was also from Abhinavagupta's grand-disciple, so he was also great.

JOHN: His master was Kṣemarāja? His immediate master was Kṣemarāja?

SWAMIJI: Yes, and Kṣemarāja's master, direct master, was Abhinavagupta.

यानं क्षितौ यानगतश्च देहो
देहेऽपि चान्यः पुरुषो निविष्टः ।
ममत्वमुर्व्यां न तथा यथा स्वे
देहेऽतिमात्रं च विमूढतैषा ॥(२५।१८)

yānaṁ kṣitau yānagataśca deho
dehe'pi cānyaḥ puruṣo niviṣṭaḥ /
mamatvamurvyāṁ na tathā yathā sve
dehe'timātraṁ ca vimūḍhataiṣā //[106]

It is said in the *Mārkaṇḍeya Purāṇa*, . . .

It is the history of Mārkaṇḍa *ṛṣi*. He has nominated the treatment of Madālasa *yoginī*, how she elevated her children.

. . . *yānaṁ kṣitau*–in Sanskrit–*yānaṁ kṣitau yānagataśca deho*, actually, O children, *yānaṁ kṣitau*, when you are riding on a *tonga* . . .

You know a *tonga*? A *tonga* is a chariot.

. . . when you are seated on a *tonga* and you are running on the roadside, on the road, and the pony is dragging this chariot, actually, *yānaṁ kṣitau*, *yānaṁ*, this *tonga* is existing on the earth, *yānagataṣca deho*, on that is seated one's body, living body, but that body is also dead. The body is not Brahma.[107]

Dehe'pi cānyaḥ puruṣo niviṣṭam, in the heart of the body, there is *puruṣa*, there is *ātma*. *Mamatvamurvyāṁ na tathā yathā sve*, actually, you ought to have developed I-ness on *pṛthvī* (earth) because the basis is the earth, that road, the pathway. On the pathway, everything is held.

And the ignorance of misunderstanding is this [that] it is *bhrānti* that we think, "this body is mine". You don't think, "this

106 *Mārkaṇḍeya Purāṇa*, 25.18.

107 That is, Brahman.

earth is mine", [i.e., the earth] where you are actually standing, where you are actually existing. You are existing on the earth, you are not existing in the body, and you misunderstand your *ātma* [to be existing] *in* [your] body. You [think] that it is existing in [your] body and you have forgotten that it is existing on *pṛthvī*.

The best way of understanding was, you ought to have inserted your I-ness on *pṛthvī*, not in the body. *Vimūḍhataiṣā*, this is the misunderstanding of everybody in this world.

Do you understand?

yānaṁ kṣitau yānagataśca deho
dehe'pi cānyaḥ puruṣo niviṣṭaḥ /
mamatvamurvyāṁ na tathā yathā sve
dehe'timātraṁ ca vimūḍhataiṣā //
[repeated]

So he says how He enwraps His own Self, real Self:

PS DVD 2 (00:53:37)

देह-प्राणविमर्शन-
धीज्ञान-नभःप्रपञ्चयोगेन ।
आत्मानं वेष्टयते
चित्रं जालेन जालकार इव ॥३२॥

deha-prāṇa-vimarśana-
dhījñāna-nabhaḥ-prapañca-yogena /
ātmānaṁ veṣṭayate
citraṁ jālena jālakāra iva //32//

Deha prāṇa vimarśana dhījñāna-nabhaḥ prapañca yogena. Deha, *prāṇa*, *vimarśana*, by the conduct of one's own body, and by the conducting process of one's breath, and by *dhījñāna*, by intellectual power, *nabhaḥ prapañca yogena*, by *śūnya pramātṛ*, who goes inside nothingness.

For instance, it is wakefulness (*deha*), dreaming state (*puryāṣṭaka*), dreamless state (*prāṇa*), and *śūnya* (void), and by expanding one's own formation in [these] four ways, *ātmānaṁ veṣṭayate*, this Lord Siva enwraps His nature.

How He enwraps [Himself]? *Citraṁ*, it is the wonder of the wonders in this world, which is not understood properly how it happens, how it works. Just like *jālena jālakāra*, just like the spider makes a web of his own production and is ultimately caught in this very web. [The spider] enwraps [itself in its web] and he dies afterwards. There is no way out for him.

Bas, now he says how this misunderstanding will be removed. For this he explains now in further *ślokas* how this misunderstanding of thinking is removed.

JOHN: The thinking that, "this body is mine"?

SWAMIJI: "This body is mine." He thinks that. By that . . . not only the [physical] body, [but] the four kinds of bodies–the body of wakefulness (*deha*), the body of the dreaming state (*puryāṣṭaka*), the body of the dreamless state (*prāṇa*), and the body of nothingness (*śūnya*).

DENISE: Voidness.

SWAMIJI: Voidness. When there is no breath, that is the body of [*śūnya*]. That is *pralayākala*; at the same time, it is *pralayākala*.[108]

So, by these four bodies, He enwraps His nature of consciousness just like a spider [does] with his own production.

katham eṣa durnivāro mahāmoho dehādi-pramātṛtāsamut-thaḥ pralīyate?–iti bhagavat-svātantryameva atra hetuḥ[109] [comm. introduction to verse 33]

It can be removed only by the free will of *bodha* Bhairava[110],

---

108 For more on *pralayākala*, see Appendix A-5, "Seven States of Perceivers".

109 "How is this great delusion, which is difficult to avoid and which arises from (identifying) the Self with the body etc., dissolved? To answer this question he says (in what follows) that here the cause is nothing but the independence of God." Paramārthasāra, John Hughes, (1972).

110 Bhairava who is all-doing (*sarvakartṛtva*) and all-knowing (*sarvajñatva*). *Bodha* Bhairava is "Bhairava [who is] filled with awareness." Swami Lakshmanjoo, *Tantrāloka* 1.122, USF archive. See also verse 16.

and by His bestowing *tīvra-tīvra śaktipāta*[111] on any one of His Selves.

PS DVD 2 (00:58:23)

स्वज्ञानविभवभासन-
योगेनोद्वेष्टयेन्निजात्मानम् ।
इति बन्धमोक्षचित्रां
क्रीडां प्रतनोति परमशिवः ॥३३॥

sva-jñāna-vibhava-bhāsana-
yogenodveṣṭayen-nijātmānam /
iti bandha-mokṣa-citrāṁ
krīḍāṁ pratanoti paramaśivaḥ //33//

Paramaśiva, Parabhairava, in fact, Parabhairava, *svajñāna vibhava bhāsana yogena*, when Parabhairava manifests His own nature, the revealing of His own nature, *udveṣṭayet nijātmānam*, according to the will of His free will, He appears in many individual beings in the form of the Parabhairava state. So, although I am Parabhairava one[112], there are at least one thousand Parabhairavas created, and they also reveal their nature and are situated in the state of Parabhairava.

And others are stuck; they are overwhelmed with absolute ignorance and darkness, and they are caught in the pangs of repeated births and deaths on the other side.

But, in fact, this section and that section–that revealed section of so many Parabhairavas and the concealed section of so many stuck Parabhairavas, brute Parabhairavas–He enjoys this drama.

Iti bandha mokṣa citrāṁ krīḍāṁ. This is the play. He creates this play showing hundreds of Parabhairavas in their revealing position. And others are stuck, and they have become brutes, *rākśasas* (demons). Those are also Parabhairavas. Those are discarded Parabhairavas. And this is the play, and He enjoys. This is His play.

END Paramārthasara DVD 2 (01:01:19)

---

111 For more on *śaktipāta*, see Appendix A-7.

112 Swamiji is referring to himself.

DVD Three

Not only this.

PS DVD 3 (00:00:04)

सृष्टि स्थिति-संहारा
जाग्रत्स्वप्नौ सुषुप्तमिति तस्मिन् ।
भान्ति तुरीये धामनि
तथापि तैर्नावृतां भाति ॥३४॥

sṛṣṭi sthiti-saṁhārā
jāgrat-svapnau suṣuptam-iti tasmin /
bhānti turīye dhāmani
tathāpi tair-nāvṛtaṁ bhāti //34//

Creation, protection, and destruction, these three. *Jāgrat* (wakefulness), *svapna* (dreaming), and *suṣupti* (dreamless sleep), these three, all of these three. [There are] other [combinations] of threes also. There are so many other threes. This is only the three-fold creation. Everywhere you will see three. The limited soul, the unlimited soul, and the medium [soul], like this.

Tasmin turīye dhāmani bhānti! But they also reside in that Parabhairava state; but the Parabhairava state is not concealed by those [limited states]. They are created by Parabhairava but, after their creation/existence, they can't enwrap Parabhairava. Parabhairava cannot be wrapped. Parabhairava wraps them in their limitation, but Parabhairava, on the contrary, Parabhairava won't be wrapped. This is His play.

Another *śloka*:

PS DVD 3 (00:01:42)

जाग्रद्विश्वं भेदात्
स्वप्नस्तेजः प्रकाशमाहात्म्यात् ।

प्राज्ञः सुप्तावस्था
ज्ञानघनत्वात्ततः परं तुर्यम् ॥३५॥

jāgrad-viśvaṁ bhedāt
svapnas-tejaḥ prakāśa-māhātmyāt /
prājñaḥ suptāvasthā
jñāna-ghanatvāt-tataḥ paraṁ turyam //35//

There are actually [four] states: *jāgrat* (wakefulness), and the dreaming state (*svapna*), and *suṣupti* (dreamless sleep), and *turya*[113] (the fourth state). [These are] four stages: *jāgrat*, *svapna*, *suṣupti*, and *turya*.

Jāgrat creates this whole differentiated world. In *jāgrat*, you will see the world which will be observed by all individuals, separatedly. When I see John Hughes at this time, George will also see, observe, John Hughes; Denise will also observe John Hughes; everybody will observe John Hughes. This is the trick in wakefulness.

And the dreaming state. When, in the dreaming state, I see John Hughes–I am dreaming and I see John Hughes in my dreaming state–George is sleeping on my side, in his own bed, [but] he won't see John Hughes; at that time, he won't see John. And Jonathan will not see John Hughes. You won't see John Hughes in your dream. So it is *teja*.[114] You should find that there in *svapna*. *Svapna* is far better than wakefulness. In wakefulness, it is *sāmanya*, equal to everybody. But the dreaming state is not equal to everybody; it is only for the individual, it is stuck in the individual. So, it is your own creation. It is not the creation of Parabhairava there. Parabhairava's creation is in *jāgrat* (wakefulness). And your own creation is just like Parabhairava in the dreaming state. In the dreaming state, you can make anything, you can create anything. You can create your own vehicles, you can create your own houses, you can create your own trees,

113 The literal meaning of *turya* is 'fourth'. For detailed explanation of *turya*, see Appendix A-13.

114 In a dream, the external senses cease to function, so the objects one perceives in a dream are created from one's own internal light (*teja*). [*Editor's note*]

pathways, people around you, etc.

"*Namaskar*! How are you, how are you?"

"Yes, yes. Go on. I am fine."

But, actually, there is nobody. He is just lying in his bed.

Who?

JOHN: That dreamer.

SWAMIJI: The dreamer. So this is special. He shows us that it is not only the specialty in Me that I create this world. You have got that power also, but in the limited circle. You can create your own world in your own bed during the night, and Viresh will create his own dreams. You will create your own creation. So it is *teja*, it is called *teja*.

Jāgrat, wakefulness, is *virāt*. *Virāt* means it is universal, i.e., everybody can perceive this. There will be not this much[115] difference between your perception or his perception in things.

But there, [in the dreaming state, everybody creates/perceives their own world]. So it is your own. It is higher than *jāgrat*.

Prājñaḥ suptāvasthā. Now, when you are in your dreamless state (*suṣupti*), when you are just dreaming nothing, then you have created a *pralaya* of your own, you have destroyed the whole universe yourself! You have got that power which I have! Parabhairava has that same power and you have also that same power in the dreamless state.

And, in *turya*, *jñāna ghanatvāttataḥ paraṁ*, in *turya*, you are just like Me. There is no difference between Parabhairava and the one who is established in *turya*.

So this is equal, i.e., outside and inside.

PS DVD 3 (00:07:02)

जलधर-धूम-रजोभि-
मलिनीक्रियते यथा न गगनतलम् ।
तद्वन्मायाविकृतिभि-
रपरामृष्टः परः पुरुषः ॥३६॥

115 Not the slightest.

jala-dhara-dhūma-rajobhir-
malinī-kriyate yathā na gagana-talam /
tadvan-māyā-vikṛtibhir-
aparāmṛṣṭaḥ paraḥ puruṣaḥ //36//

He gives an example now [to illustrate] what is the difference between ignorance and knowledge; what is the difference between being posted in the Parabhairava state and being posted in the disgusted, trodden state of the *jīva*[116]. He gives an example for that.

Jala dhara dhūma rajobhir malinī kriyate yathā na gagana talam. Jala dhara, by heaps of clouds–this *ākāśa*[117], which is quite blue and crystal-blue always–if heaps of clouds come, they cannot affect this vast *ākāśa*. This vast *ākāśa* cannot get soaked in these clouds. *Dhūma*, if you burn the whole world, and there will be lots of smoke, and *ākāśa* will not be perceived by anybody at that time, but, in fact, *ākāśa* is great. [It] cannot be smoked, soaked in smoke. [It] is again that crystal-like blue.

In the same way, *māyā vikṛtibhir*, by this tossing here and there, and shooting here and there, of these rascals[118] (this is *māyā vikṛtibhir*; these are the crooked ways of *māyā*), *para puruṣa* (Parabhairava) cannot be . . .

JONATHAN: Stained?

SWAMIJI: Not stained.

. . . cannot be confused. He won't get any confusion. He will remain just like the *ākāśa*.

Parabhairava does not care if so many things happen in this world. He waits for the time when He likes [and] "*brut*", at once, all is finished and there is only Parabhairava. So Parabhairava does not care for all of these dances, fruitless dances.

JOHN: But they are His dances. They are His dances. These fruitless dances are His play.

SWAMIJI: They are His dances but He does not care, He does not [care to] end it at once. [On the contrary], we are just limited

116 Limited individual.

117 Ether or space. In this instance, *ākāśa* means the sky.

118 Here, Swamiji was referring to the state of social unrest that was prevaling in Kashmir during 1990. [*Editor's note*]

beings, so we are in threat, [wondering] how it will be crossed over.

PS DVD 3 (00:10:47)

एकस्मिन् घटगगने
रजसा व्याप्ते, भवन्ति नान्यानि ।
मलिनानि, तद्वदेते
जीवाः सुख-दुःखभेदजुषः ॥३७॥

ekasmin ghaṭa-gagane
rajasā vyāpte, bhavanti nānyāni /
malināni, tadvadete
jīvāḥ sukha-duḥkha-bheda-juṣaḥ //37//[119]

In the same way, *jivaḥ sukha duḥkha bhu*, some individuals are happy, some individuals are [feeling] painful, some individuals are stuck in *ājñāna* (ignorance), *moha* (forgetfulness), stuck in snoring, some are in those mosquitoes. Those are also Parabhairava. That is "stuck-Parabhairava". And, at the time of being stuck also, He is unstuck. He enjoys this also!

DENISE: The stuck-ness.

SWAMIJI: Yes.

PS DVD 3 (00:11:38)

शान्ते शान्त इवायं
हृष्टे हृष्टो विमोहवति मूढः ।
तत्त्वगणे सति भगवान्
न पुनः परमार्थतः स तथा ॥३८॥

119 "(Just as) when the air contained in a single pot is full of dust, and other portions of air contained in other pots do not become dirtied, so likewise, these limited individuals enjoy the diversity of happiness and unhappiness." John Hughes, *Paramārthsāra* (1972).

śānte śānta ivāyaṁ
hṛṣṭe hṛṣto vimohavati mūḍhaḥ /
tattva-gaṇe sati bhagavān
na punaḥ paramārthataḥ sa tathā //38//

When *tattva gaṇe*, this elementary world, is *sante*, [in its] appeased state, there is *pralaya* (destruction), there is nothing, only water, *bas*. From *pṛthvī tattva* to that . . .

Which one?

DENISE: *Śānta* . . .

SWAMIJI: . . . *śāntātīta kalā*[120], all *tattva gaṇas*[121] are *śānta*, appeased.

What is the position of Parabhairava there? If you ask, "How is Parabhairava existing [there]?" Parabhairava is existing, *bas*, appeased! Parabhairava is appeased there. Parabhairava is appeased in the appeased elementary world, the thirty-six elementary world.

Parabhairava is furious in the furious [state of] these one hundred and eighteen worlds. When one hundred and eighteen worlds become furious, that is *pralaya* (destruction), crashing with each other. [At] that time, Parabhairava is like that.

But, in fact, Parabhairava is neither this nor that. He is above also, and watching this play of His own Self. *Na punaḥ paramārthataḥ sa tathā*, but, in fact, in the real sense, He is not like that. He is above that. He is that, He is not that, He is above that–three ways. Even more: He is not-not that, He is not-not-not-not that, He is the negation of that, He is the affirmation of that.

You can't imagine how He does, and His play is out of our limited vision. You cannot visualize that. No, the limited soul cannot visualize that although, at that very moment, Parabhairava visualizes that! [Although] you say that, "It is not visualized", [still] it is visualized! In the state of not being visualized [by you], it is visualized [at that very moment] by another being of His. There are so many giants of Parabhairava. One is this, one is this, one is this, one is this [Swamiji pulls many faces]. You cannot [imagine how many there are]. It is wonderful!

---

120 For an explanation of the five *kalās*, see Appendix A-8.

121 The assembly (*gaṇa*) of all the elements (*tattvas*). [*Editor's note*]

PS DVD 3 (00:14:42)

यदनात्मन्यपि तद्रूपा-
वभासमं तत् पुरा निराकृत्य ।
आत्मन्यनात्मरूपां
भ्रान्तिं विदलयति परमात्मा ॥३९॥

yad-anātmany-api tad-rūpā-
vabhāsanaṁ tat purā nirākṛtya /
ātmany-anātma-rūpāṁ
bhrāntiṁ vidalayati paramātmā //39//

When there is *bhram* (*bhram* means "misunderstanding"), when misunderstanding is manifested all over the world, that is called *bhrānti*, misunderstanding everywhere.

This *bhrānti*, *yat anātmanyapi tadrūpa avabhāsamaṁ*, that *bhrānti*, He creates that *bhrānti*, He manifests that *bhrānti*. Then, by His own free choice, at the same time, He destroys that *bhrānti*, and there is no *bhrānti*. To Him, nothing has happened; if there is *pralaya*[122], nothing has happened. It is Your own will.

JOHN: So, actually, from the real point of view, it's all perfect.

SWAMIJI: Huh?

JOHN: Actually, it is perfect.

SWAMIJI: Actually, with the whole, when you vasten your vision beyond time, beyond space, beyond form, then you will come to this conclusion that it is all perfect, everywhere, every time.

PS DVD 3 (00:16:25)

इत्थं विभ्रमयुगलक-
समूलविच्छेदने कृतार्थस्य ।

122 The literal meaning of *pralaya* is dissolution or absorption. Generally *pralaya* is used in the sense of the end of an era, or destruction of the world. [*Editor's note*]

कर्तव्यान्तरकलना
न जातु परयोगिनो भवति ॥४०॥

itthaṁ vibhrama-yugalaka-
samūla-viccedane kṛtārthasya /
kartavyāntara-kalanā
na jātu parayogino bhavati //40//

This way, that [person] who is *para yogina*, who is established in the *yoga* of the supreme Bhairava, although he creates *bhrānti*, he discards *bhrānti* with his Parabhairava effort. Then, nothing remains for him to do. He has done what was to be done. He has gained what was to be gained. He has done everything. So he has nothing remaining to be done. He is full, and he is always full.

JOHN: I think *bhrānti* is "illusion".

SWAMIJI: Illusion, yes, that is misunderstanding. Illusion cannot be [discarded] because illusion is [that] which is always there.

JOHN: No. Sometimes, say for example, this example of when you are in the desert, and you look ahead and you see some town and you think that town is there, and you drive along and all of a sudden that goes away, that is *bhrānti*.

DENISE: Mirage.

JOHN: Mirage, that mirage which comes up, and you drive along, and it goes away, that is *bhrānti*.

SWAMIJI: Yes, yes.

JOHN: We call that "illusion".

SWAMIJI: Illusion?

JOHN: You think something is there, and it's not there.

PS DVD 3 (00:18:02)

पृथिवी प्रकृतिर्माया
त्रितयमिदं वेद्यरूपतापतितम् ।

अद्वैतभावनबलाद्
भवति हि सन्मात्रपरिशेषम् ॥४१॥

pṛthivī prakṛtir-māyā
tritayam-idaṁ vedya-rūpatā-patitam /
advaita-bhāvana-balād
bhavati hi sanmātra-pariśeṣam //41//

Pṛthivī, *prakṛti*, and *māyā*, not [the *tattvas*] above [*māyā*], these three which are in the lower planes of creation, . . .

Pṛthivī is *bedha*, *prakṛti* is *bedhābedha*, and *māyā* is above that. *Māyā* is *abheda*[123], but *māyā* is nothingness. *Pṛthivī* is *jāgrat* (wakefulness), *prakṛti* is *svapna* (dreaming), and *māyā* is *suṣupti* (the dreamless state), when there is no creation of any thoughts.

. . . these three are *vedya rūpatāpatitam*, these are living in the objective field of the world. This is the objective field. *Advaita ātma balāt*, when you insert the undifferentiated state of Parabhairava in them and soak these three in the Parabhairava state, *bhavati hi sanmātra pariśeṣam*, this whole world becomes one with Parabhairava. It has no difference at all, there. It is knowledge. That is called "elevation". This elevation and [delusion], both are functioning; both ways this is functioning. This creation of the world is functioning in both ways, elevation and delusion.

He gives now another example:

PS DVD 3 (00:20:21)

रशनाकुण्डलकटकं
भेदत्यागेन दृश्यते यथा हेम ।
तद्वद्भेदत्यागे
सन्मात्रं सर्वमाभाति ॥४२॥

123 *Bedha* (differentiated), *bedhābheda* (differentiated-cum-undifferentiated), *abheda* (undifferentiated). [*Editor's note*]

raśanā-kuṇḍala-kaṭakaṁ
bheda-tyāgena dṛśyate yathā hema /
tadvad-bheda-tyāge
sanmātraṁ sarvam-ābhāti //42//

Raśanā, that of golden . . . what?

DENISE: Garland?

SWAMIJI: Garland, which you had, that *mālā*.

DENISE: Oh, necklace?

SWAMIJI: Not necklace.

DENISE: With beads, *mālā*, I have that.

SWAMIJI: *Kuṇḍala* means earrings. *Kaṭakaṁ* . . .

DENISE: Bracelet?

SWAMIJI: [Swamiji indicates in the affirmative]

When there is a goldsmith, you ask the goldsmith: "What is the cost of this *mālā*? I would like to sell it. Will you purchase it?" The goldsmith won't care for the *mālā*. The goldsmith won't care for the earrings. The goldsmith won't care for these [bracelets]. He will care for the gold. He will care for the quantity of gold. He will put it on the scale and see how heavy this is of gold and he will put the cost according to the [weight of] gold. He will not put the cost according to the beauty of that ornament.

Tadvad bhedatyāge, in the same way, *bheda tyāge*, if you say, "This woman is beautiful", [or] "This woman is ugly", [or] "This woman is brute way", [or] "This woman is just *pagal* (mad)", [or] "This woman is [Swamiji demonstrates]", like this, leave this aside–the womanhood is the same! *Tadvad bheda tyāge sanmātraṁ sarvamābhāti*, when you leave aside this differentiated perception, undifferentiated Being will appear to you.

PS DVD 3 (00:23:00)

तद्ब्रह्म परं शुद्धं
शान्तमभेदात्मकं समं सकलम् ।
अमृतं सत्यं शक्तौ-
विश्राम्यति भास्वरूपायाम् ॥४३॥

इष्यत इति वेद्यत इति
 संपाद्यत इति च भास्वरूपेण ।
आपरामृष्टं यदपि तु
 नभःप्रसूनत्वमभ्येति ॥४४॥
शक्तित्रिशूलपरिगम-
 योगेन समस्तमपि परमेशे ।
शिवनामनि परमार्थे
 विसृज्यते देवदेवेन ॥४५॥

tad-brahma paraṁ śuddhaṁ
śāntam-abhedātmakaṁ samaṁ sakalam /
amṛtaṁ satyaṁ śaktau-
viśrāmyati bhā-svarūpāyām //43//
iṣyata iti vedyata iti
saṁpādyata iti ca bhā-svarūpeṇa /
āparāmṛṣṭaṁ yadapi tu
nabhaḥ-prasūnatvam-abhyeti //44//
śakti-triśūla-parigama-
yogena samastam-api parameśe /
śiva-nāmani paramārthe
visṛjyate deva-devena //45//

These are three *ślokas* connected with each other. These are the forty-third, forty-fourth, and forty-fifth *ślokas*. In these, he explains the three courses, three sections, of this whole world which is created.

One section is created in the *bheda* state, the differentiated state; one section is created partly differentiated and partly undifferentiated, medium (*bhedābheda*); and another is undifferentiated (*abheda*)–*bheda*, *bhedābheda*, and *abheda*. In this way, this world is created.

But, in fact, the creation of *bheda*, the creation of *bhedābheda*, and the creation of *abheda* are just one. They are only *parā abheda*. There is *parā abheda*, supreme *abheda*. Supreme *abheda* means [that] which is more than undifferentiated. From that Being, these three different things appear, are manifested.

One is undifferentiated, one is . . .

DENISE: Undifferentiated in difference.

SWAMIJI: Undifferentiated?

DENISE: One is undifferentiated.

SWAMIJI: Yes. These three ways of creation are created by that super-undifferentiated state of Parabhairava.

So, you must not think that Parabhairava is away from you. He is always there and always craving for you to have Him! If you don't want to have Him–it is your choice–no matter, that is also fine. That is also your own way of thinking. Don't have Him. Enjoy hells. That is also enjoyment. And you are never [away from Him]. You are caught by that grip. You are grabbed by Him, always.

And this is the *krīḍa* (play) in *bheda*, in *bhedābheda*, and in *abheda*. This three-fold [play] is *krīḍa prataṇoti paramaśiva*[124]. And who is handling [it]? That Parabhairava is handling this *krīḍa*.

पुनरपि च पञ्चशक्ति-
प्रसरणक्रमेण बहिरपि तत् ।
अण्डत्रयं विचित्रं
सृष्टं बहिरात्मलाभेन ॥४६॥

punar-api ca pañca-śakti-
prasaraṇa-krameṇa bahir-api tat /
aṇḍa-trayaṁ vicitraṁ
sṛṣṭaṁ bahir-ātma-lābhena //46//[125]
[not recited or translated]

---

124 *Krīḍa prataṇoti paramaśiva* means this play (*krīḍa*) is the undertaking (*prataṇoti*) of Parabhairava (*paramaśiva*). [*Editor's note*]

125 "And once again this triad of spheres is created outside also in the process of pouring forth of the five *śaktis* (energies) by objectivating the Self." *Paramārthasāra*, John Hughes (1972).

PS DVD 3 (00:26:24)

इति शक्तिचक्रयन्त्रं
    क्रीडायोगेन वाहयन्देवः ।
अहमेव शुद्धरूपः
    शक्तिमहाचक्रनायकपदस्थः ॥४७॥
मय्येव भाति विश्वं
    दर्पण इव निर्मले घटादीनि ।
मत्तः प्रसरति सर्वं
    स्वप्नविचित्रत्वमिव सुप्तात् ॥४८॥
अहमेव विश्वरूपः
    करचरणादिस्वभाव इव देहः ।
सर्वस्मिन्नहमेव
    स्फुरामि भावेषु भास्वरूपमिव ॥४९॥

iti śakti-cakra-yantraṁ
    krīḍā-yogena vāhayan-devaḥ /
aham-eva śuddha-rūpaḥ
    śakti-mahā-cakra-nāyaka-padasthaḥ //47//
mayyeva bhāti viśvaṁ
    darpaṇa iva nirmale ghaṭādīni /
mattaḥ prasarati sarvaṁ
    svapna-vicitratvam-iva suptāt //48//
aham-eva viśva-rūpaḥ
    kara-caraṇādi-svabhāva iva dehaḥ /
sarvasminn-aham-eva
    sphurāmi bhāveṣu bhā-svarūpamiva //49//
[Verses 47, 48, 49 not translated in full.][126]

126 47. Thus I alone, God, propel the device of the wheel of *śaktis*, standing as the controller of the great wheel of *śaktis*. 48. In me alone the universe shines like objects in an unspotted mirror. The universe emerges from me like the diversity of a dream from the (state of) deep

This way, *śakticakra yantraṁ*, this is a big wheel, this *cakra* of His unlimited energies. Unlimited energies are the spokes of this *cakra*. And this *cakra*, He is playing this *cakra*.

The first player comes in the drama of *mātṛkā cakra*. *Mātṛkā cakra* means from [the letter] '*a*' to '*ha*'–"*ahaṁ*" (there is also "*ahaṁ*"[127]). '*A*' is the first letter and '*ha*' is the last letter. This is the first *śakti-cakra*; this is *mātṛkā cakra*[128].

Another *śakti-cakra* is *pratibimba vāda*, reflection, the [doctrine] of reflection.[129] This whole universe is the reflection of Parabhairava! You will see [that] nothing is existing which is not existing in the Parabhairava state. Nothing is here, not even one straw of grass also, that you will find is not there. That straw is also there, and then you will find it here.

So, Parabhairava is not far away from you. He is here. He is universal. Everything that is shining here, it is shining there.

> [The first *śakti-cakra*] is *mātṛkā cakra* and another is reflection, *pratibimba vāda*.
>
> And, in [the explanation of] *śāmbhāvopāya* in the third

---

sleep. 49. I alone am the universe, like a body consists of hands, feet, etc. And I alone flash forth as this universe like the nature of light in things. *Paramārthasāra*, John Hughes (1972).

127 "*Ahaṁ* is I-consciousness, I-consciousness which is manifested. . . . '*A*' indicates the state of Lord Śiva, '*ha*' indicates the state of Śakti, and '*ma*' indicates the state of individuality–Lord Śiva, Śakti, and the individual. So, "*ahaṁ*" is the journey, outside journey. "*Ma-ha-a*" is the internal journey, returning journey; you return to your own nature there. When you return to your own nature, the *mantra* is "*ma-ha-a*". And when you travel outside from your nature, then it is "*ahaṁ*"–'*a*' in the first, '*ha*' is in the center, and '*ma*' is the indication of individuality, outside." Swami Lakshmanjoo, *Parātrīśikā Vivaraṇa*, USF archive.

128 "*Mātṛkā cakra* is the theory of the alphabet. This theory teaches us that the whole universe is created by God, Lord Śiva, as one with, and not separated from, His own nature." *Kashmir Shaivism–The Secret Supreme*, 3.15-28.

129 "This theory teaches [advanced *yogīs*] how to be aware in their daily activities–while talking, while walking, while tasting, while touching, while hearing, while smelling. While they are performing all of these various actions, they see that all of these actions move in their supreme consciousness. . . . This is the awareness that comes from the practice of *pratibimba*." Ibid., 4.29-32.

āhnika of *Tantrāloka*, these three aspects are explained–only these three aspects. Which aspects?

The first is *mātṛkā cakra*, and *mātṛkā cakra* is from [the letter] '*a*' to '*ha*'–the theory of alphabets (in the *Parātrīṁśika Vivaraṇa* also, you will find the same). And then another process is of *pratibimba vāda*, reflection. [The universe] is the reflection of Parabhairava. And another aspect is *ahaṁ parāmarśa* (*ahaṁ*, "I am this").

JOHN: So those are the three aspects that are explained in the third *āhnika*?

SWAMIJI: Vedānta?

JOHN: No, third *āhnika*.

SWAMIJI: Yes, the third *āhnika*. And *Parātrīṁśika Vivaraṇa* also, in the *Parātrīṁśika Vivaraṇa* also.

GEORGE: So that "*ahaṁ*" is *śakti-cakra*?

SWAMIJI: "*Ahaṁ*" is also *śakti-cakra*, yes.

JOHN: "*Ma-ha-a*" doesn't play in this?

SWAMIJI: ["*Ma-ha-a*" is the] withdrawal form. Exposing and withdrawing.

JOHN: *Saṅkoca* (contraction) and *vikāsa* (expansion)?

SWAMIJI: And [inaudible], whatever will be joined in that [laughter]. You know that?

JOHN: Say again, sir?

SWAMIJI: This and that, this and that.

JOHN: Squeezing and . . .

SWAMIJI: Yes. It is all one!
[To Viresh] Why do you laugh?

VIRESH: I thought he was going to say, you know . . .

SWAMIJI: [laughs]

द्रष्टा श्रोता घ्राता
देहेन्द्रियवर्जितोऽप्यकर्तापि ।

सिद्धान्तागमतर्कां
श्चित्रानहमेव रचयामि ॥५०॥

draṣṭā śrotā ghrātā
dehendriya-varjito'py-akartāpi /
siddhāntāgama-tarkāṁś
citrān-aham-eva racayāmi //50//
[verse not recited or translated][130]

PS DVD 3 (00:31:28)

इत्थं द्वैतविकल्पे
गलिते प्रविलङ्घ्य मोहनीं मायाम् ।
सलिले सलिलं क्षीरे
क्षीरमिव ब्रह्मणि लयी स्यात् ॥५१॥

itthaṁ dvaita-vikalpe
galite pravilaṅghya mohanīṁ māyām /
salile salilaṁ kṣīre
kṣīram-iva brahmaṇi layī syāt //51//

In this way, *dvaita vikalpe galite*, when differentiated perception–and the threat of differentiated perception–the threat of differentiated perception is *galite*, is finished, is totally destroyed, *pravilaṅghya mohanīṁ māyām*, and *mohanīṁ māyā* also (i.e., ignorance, misunderstanding), and [when you know that] this [ignorance] is not the actual position, then *salile salilaṁ*, just as water is diluted in water [or] milk is diluted in milk, in the same way, this whole universe will be diluted in Parabhairava.

130 "I am the seer, I am the hearer, I am the smeller, although I am without bodily organs. And although I am not their composer, yet I alone create the various schools, scriptures, and philosophical arguments." *Paramārthasāra*, John Hughes (1972).

इत्थं तत्त्वसमूहे
भावनया शिवमयत्वमभियाते ।
कः शोकः को मोहः
सर्वं ब्रह्मावलोकयतः ॥५२॥

ittham tattva-samūhe
bhāvanayā śiva-mayatvam-abhiyāte /
kaḥ śokaḥ ko mohaḥ
sarvaṁ brahmāvalokayataḥ / /52/ /
[not recited or translated][131]

PS DVD 3 (00:32:41)

कर्मफलं शुभमशुभं
मिथ्याज्ञानेन संगमादेव ।
विषमो हि सङ्गदोष-
स्तस्करयोगोऽप्यतस्करस्येव ॥५३॥

karma-phalaṁ śubham-aśubhaṁ
mithyājñānena saṁgamād-eva /
viṣamo hi saṅga-doṣas-
taskara-yogo'py-ataskarasyeva / /53/ /

This is the theory of *karma*, the theory of actions, which bear fruit (*karma phalam*). It is good and bad; it is always good and bad. Actions, all actions, [that] are being done, they are always bearing good fruit and bad fruit.

But it is because of association with brutes, when Parabhairava is associated with brutes, with *rākṣasas* (demons). He has

131 "And when the aggregate of *tattvas* has thus become intergrated into Śiva through awareness, then what grief or what delusion could be for one beholding the universe as Brahman?" *Paramārthasāra*, John Hughes (1972).

made friendship with *rākṣasas* because of His own choice. *Viṣamo hi saṅgadoṣa*, Parabhairava is a devil! Parabhairava has become a devil in the market. Parabhairava is to be shot down–this Parabhairava. And that also is observed by Parabhairava in the upper level. Not [only] in that upper level [but] in the lower level also.

JOHN: So Parabhairava is shooting Parabhairava?

SWAMIJI: Yes, shooting-Parabhairava and shot-Parabhairava, at the same time.

JOHN: And the means of shooting also.

SWAMIJI: The means of shooting and . . .

JOHN: *Pramāṇa, prameya, pramātṛ* . . .

SWAMIJI: Yes.

JOHN: . . . and *pramiti.*[132]

SWAMIJI:

PS DVD 3 (00:34:24)

लोकव्यवहारकृतां
ये इहाविद्यामुपासते मूढाः ।
ते यान्ति जन्ममृत्यू
धर्माधर्मार्गलाबद्धाः ॥५४॥

loka-vyavahāra-kṛtāṁ
ye ihāvidyām-upāsate mūḍhāḥ /
te yānti janma-mṛtyū
dharmādharmārgalā-baddhāḥ //54//

Those brutes who treat with respect, with great behavior, ignorance, dull ignorance–those people who respect and behave faithfully with attachment [to] this ignorance, those brutes are sentenced to fearful hells, dirty hells. Those are sentenced to [those hells and then they cry], "*Aaaaah, aaaaah*! Who will uplift

132 *Pramāṇa* (cognitive), *prameya* (objective), *pramātṛ* (subjective), and *pramiti* (supreme subjective). For a further explanation, see Appendix A-15.

me here? Who will take me out [of here]? I am gone! *Aaaaa-aaaaaah!*" And Parabhairava is also enjoying that! This is what happens in this world.

It is their own way of doing. Nobody is responsible. He is responsible. Parabhairava is responsible. What then [if He is] responsible? Who will put Him to task? Who will investigate Him? Nobody! He is Himself the investigator of all. He is not to be investigated. Nobody has the guts to investigate Him because there is no one [other] than Parabhairava existing anywhere. He is everywhere.

GEORGE: Like I took this wretched bus ride. That was my doing.

SWAMIJI: Yes, it was your choice.

PS DVD 3 (00:36:21)

अज्ञानकालनिचितं
धर्माधर्मात्मकं तु कर्मापि ।
चिरसंचितमिव तूलं
नश्यति विज्ञानदीप्तिवशात् ॥५५॥

ajñāna-kāla-nicitaṁ
dharmādharmātmakaṁ tu karmāpi /
cira-saṁcitam-iva tūlaṁ
naśyati vijñāna-dīpti-vaśāt //55//

When the time comes for Parabhairava to remain in His . . . Parabhairava, when He likes to be established in His own nature, He then collects all this fuel of the universe–the wretched universe, which is just not worth having; He thinks that it is not worth having now–*bas*, He collects it, and makes all cotton heaps and [ignites it] . . .

GEORGE: Matches. He lights it.

SWAMIJI: Yes, and matches.

. . . by His awareness (the awareness of Parabhairava is the matches). He burns it and then there is no nomination, no impression, no thought, nothing, as if nothing had happened. There is only Parabhairava, Parabhairava, *bas*, Parabhairava. Nothing remains in the background, nothing. There is no space, no time, nothing, no formation. There is only that God consciousness, not with a body, [but with] that *spanda*[133]. *Spanda* only remains there, everywhere. Not "everywhere". It is only *spanda*. There is no space. There is no wood, there is no carved wood, nothing. There are not these houses–they disappear. There is only *spanda* then left.

Then, when this *spanda* is too much functioning, then He creates this world again. What? When it overflows, [when] His *spanda* overflows, this overflow means that there is another new creation of the world.[134] And there will be Rāmarāja.[135] At that time, there will be Rāmarāja. And you will see, one by one, you

---

133 "The element of *spanda* is that being of God consciousness in which this whole universe exists and from which this whole universe comes out. . . . And [God consciousness] is not only the resting place of the universe, this is the *prasara sthana* also, the flowing energy; this universe comes out from that. . . . It *has* to exist in God consciousness and it is coming out from God consciousness *in* God consciousness, because there is no other space for the universe to exist." Swami Lakshmanjoo, *Parātrīśikā Vivaraṇa* audio, USF archive. For more on *spanda*, see Appendix A-14.

134 "When it overflows, then you want to disconnect it. That is His position; disconnected because of too much of it [i.e., *spanda*, *ānanda*, *svātantrya*]. You want to get disconnected from that state and then [again] connect yourself, [then] it gives pleasure. That is *svātantrya*. This is why this whole universe is created. Otherwise, there was no reason to create this universe when God was there already in His own knowledge, completely. This differentiation has come out because of that overflowing of that God consciousness. The ecstasy of God consciousness is overflowing and then this happened to His own nature.

"Look at [a child]. When he is too much excited, he jumps, he hits his head. In the same way, God has done this. He has crushed His own nature because of too much of ecstasy. He wants to disconnect that ecstasy. But that ecstasy in its real way cannot be disconnected at all. He knows that. But still, for fun, He disconnects this for the time being. And, at the time of again realizing His own nature, He feels that It was already there." Swami Lakshmanjoo, *Bodhapañcadaśikā*, USF archive.

135 King Rāma, the seventh incarnation of Lord Viṣṇu, is often invoked as an example of the perfect leader. During his reign, there was said to have existed an ideal society. [*Editor's note*]

will see Rāmarāja.

PS DVD 3 (00:39:16)

ज्ञानप्राप्तौ कृतमपि
न फलाय ततोऽस्य जन्म कथम् ।
गतजन्मबन्धयोगो
भाति शिवार्कः स्वदीधितिभिः ॥५६॥

jñāna-prāptau kṛtam-api
na phalāya tato'sya janma katham /
gata-janma-bandha-yogo
bhāti śivārkaḥ sva-dīdhitibhiḥ //56//
[not recited or translated][136]

तुष-कम्बुक-किंशारुक-
मुक्तं बीजं यथाङ्कुरं कुरुते ।
नैव, तथाणवमाया-
कर्मविमुक्तो भवाङ्कुरं ह्यात्मा ॥५७॥

tuṣa-kambhuka-kiṁśāruka-
muktaṁ bījaṁ yathāṅkuraṁ kurute /
naiva, tathāṇava-māyā-
karma-vimukto bhavāṅkuraṁ hy-ātmā //57//

Just as *bījam*, any seed (*tuṣa* means the husk; *kambhuka* means that medium covering; *kiṁśāruka* means gross husk), *muktaṁ bījam*, if it is separated from these three, this, any seed, *bhavāṅkuram yathā na kurute*, it does not *aṅkuram kurute*, it

136 "In the attainment of enlightenment, his acts do not bear fruit, therefore how can there be birth for him. Since the bondage of birth has departed from him, he shines as the sun with his own rays, free of the bondage of birth, in the form of Śiva." *Paramārthasāra*, John Hughes (1972).

does not produce a sprout.

In the same way, *āṇāva karma vimukto*, *āṇavamala*, *mayīyamala*, and *kārmamala*, these three *malas* (impurities)–one is the subtlest *mala* (that is *āṇavamala*), *mayīyamala* is the medium *mala*, and *kārmamala* is the gross *mala*–[from] these three *malas*[137], if once the individual soul is separated, *na bhavāṅkuram kurute*, it won't produce repeated births and deaths. He is totally freed from the pangs of repeated births and deaths. He is just like Parabhairava.

PS DVD 3 (00:41:09)

आत्मज्ञो न कुतश्चन
    बिभेति, सर्वं हि तस्य निजरूपम् ।
नैव च शोचति, यस्मात्
    परमार्थे नाशिता नास्ति ॥५८॥

ātma-jño na kutaścana
    bibheti, sarvaṁ hi tasya nija-rūpam /
naiva ca śocati, yasmāt
    paramārtthe nāśitā nāsti //58//

Ātmajña, he who has realized one's own Self, *na kutaścana bibheti*, he does not get afraid of anybody.

Why he does not get afraid of anybody?

Sarvaṁ hi tasya nijarūpam, because His branches are everywhere scattered. You cannot get afraid of yourself.

DENISE: Yes, because He is everybody.

SWAMIJI: Yes, He is expanded; He has manifested His nature in every being. From [whom] will he get afraid?

Naiva ca śocati, and he does not get depressed also. When, amongst His manifestation, one passes away, one individual passes away, *naiva ca śocati*, he does not allow grief to agitate his being. *Yasmāt*, why? *Paramārtthe nāśitā* [*nāsti*], actually nobody dies. It is all one's manifestation and one's drama.

---

137 For an explanation of the *malas*, see Appendix A-3. See also *Kashmir Shaivism–The Secret Supreme*, 7.47-49.

Now, Yogarāja puts in his commentary an example from the *Utpalastotrāvalī* of the *Saṁgraha Stotra*[138]:

योऽविकल्पमिदमर्थमण्डलं
पश्यतीश निखिलं भवद्वपुः ।
स्वात्मपक्षपरिपूरिते जग-
त्यस्य नित्यसुखिनः कुतो भयम् ॥

yo'vikalpam-idam-artha-maṇḍalaṁ
paśyatīśa nikhilaṁ bhavad-vapuḥ /
svātma-pakṣa-paripūrite jagat-
yasya nitya-sukhinaḥ kuto bhayam //[139]

Any person who, O Lord, observes this whole universe one-pointedly, he who observes this world one-pointedly, and realizes that this is the glamour of Your manifestation, this whole universe is the glamour of Your manifestation, he is actually situated in Your manifestation, or in his own manifestation. So he is always appeased and peaceful. *Kuto bhayam*, from [whom or what] will he get afraid? There is no other [than] his being.

One gets afraid from the opposite thing when there is no opposite thing at all existing.

Granthakāro'pi, Abhinavagupta has also penned down–Yogarāja says–the author of this *Paramārthasāra* has also penned down one *śloka* somewhere. He does not know where [it is] from, but it is of Abhinavagupta.

एककोऽहमिति संसृतौ जन-
स्त्रासमाहसरसेन खिद्यते ।

138 The *Sivastotrāvalī* of Utpaladeva. The thirteenth chapter is known as the *Saṁgraha Stotra*. Utpaladeva was the disciple of Somānanda, who reintroduced the Pratyabhijña System in Kashmir. Utpaladeva was the master of Lakṣmaṇagupta, who was the master of Abhinavagupta. [*Editor's note*]

139 *Śivastotrāvalī*, 13.16.

एककोऽहमिति कोऽपरोऽस्ति मे
इत्थमस्मि गतभीर्व्यवस्थितः ॥

ekako'hamiti saṁsṛtau janas-
trāsasāhasarasena khidyate /
ekako'hamiti ko'paro'sti me
ittham-asmi gata-bhīr-vyavasthitaḥ / /

"Oh, I am alone here! I am alone! What shall I do? I am alone, *iti saṁsṛtau*, in this world."

Janaḥ, an ordinary man, if he is the only one man in Neal, if there is only one man who is not dead, all [others] are dead, all are shot down, and there is nothing, and he is the one person now saved, and he sees houses and everything, varieties of houses, and no one living. It also happens in this world.

"*Ekako'ham*, so I am alone!"

Saṁsṛtau, in this field of ignorance, *janaḥ*, that limited being, *trāsa sāhasarasena khidyate*, he is [crying], "Somebody will eat me. Somebody will come around at night time and he will [eat me]." And he closes the door in which he is living although there is nobody outside. There is no eagle, there are no dogs barking, nobody, but he is still afraid. He gets afraid still. He says, "Maybe somebody will come and eat me."

Trāsa sāhasarasena, and he is nowhere. He has got sleepless nights, sleepless days. And he cannot digest his food also. He cannot prepare his food also. Because he is alone! What he will prepare? How he will prepare? This is [the limited individual's] position.

Abhinavagupta says, "Now, look at me, what I think. I also say, 'I am alone'. *Ekako'hamiti ko'paro'sti me*, I also perceive that I am only alone, I am only one."

Who says?

Abhinavagupta says, "I am only one. *Ko'paraḥ asti me*, who is other than me existing in this whole universe?" Although he sees varieties of people, varieties of dogs, varieties of eagles, varieties of demons, although he sees, but he perceives them as not separate from his being.

Do you understand?

DENISE: As the expansion of his own nature.

SWAMIJI: His own Self.

DENISE: His own Self.

SWAMIJI: Nature? Not nature! His own Self. It is the expansion of his own Self.

How one can . . . you cannot get afraid of Viresh! If Viresh is sleeping in your bed and you will have sleepless nights–why? Viresh is your own expansion. Why should you get afraid of John? If he is sleeping with you, then will he also eat you?

DENISE: I don't think so.

SWAMIJI: Yes.

"*Itthamasmi*, in the same way, in the same manner, I am situated in this world, *gatabhīr*, without threat, without threat."

Another one:

PS DVD 3 (00:49:31)

अतिगूढहृदयगञ्ज-
प्ररूढपरमार्थरत्नसंचयतः ।
अहमेवेति महेश्वर-
भावे का दुर्गतिः कस्य ॥५९॥

atigūḍha-hṛdaya-gañja-
prarūḍha-paramārtha-ratna-saṁcayataḥ /
ahameveti maheśvara-
bhāve kā durgatiḥ kasya //59//

[That] which is innermost, secretly-existing, the treasure of the knowledge of Parabhairava–the knowledge of Parabhairava is the treasure which is secretly placed in the center of your heart, which is the universal center–and when you open that [lock] of that treasure, and *paramārtha ratna* (*paramārtha ratna* means the "jewelry of God consciousness", "the jewelry of Parabhairava"), the jewelry of Parabhairava comes from that, one by one, one by one, with varieties.

He sees one jewel–Viresh; one jewel, another jewel–this; another jewel–George; another jewel–me; another jewel–all this universe (*paramārtha ratna saṁcayataḥ*). *Aham-eveti maheśvara bhāve*, and he perceives that all these varieties of jewelry are just the manifestation of my being.

Kā durgatiḥ kasya, how will he be overwhelmed by poverty? He is the God of gods. He has got the wealth of wealth. The secret of wealth, he owns. So there is no need for him to maintain bank accounts in each and every bank of the world. He has this first-class bank account, which is not, by spending, which is not . . .

JOHN: Exhausted.

SWAMIJI: . . . which does not exhaust. And, on the contrary, which is as it is–full.

Another *śloka*:

PS DVD 3 (00:52:47)

मोक्षस्य नैव किंचिद्
धामास्ति, न चापिगमनमन्यत्र ।
अज्ञानग्रन्थिभिदा
स्वशक्त्यभिव्यक्तता मोक्षः ॥ ६० ॥

mokṣasya naiva kiṁcid
dhāmāsti, na cāpi-gamanam-anyatra /
ajñāna-granthi-bhidā
sva-śakty-abhivyaktatā mokṣaḥ / /60/ /

Actually, the liberation from repeated births and deaths and being centered in the Parabhairava state, that Parabhairava state is called "*mokṣa*". And that *mokṣa* is not somewhere in the uppermost *ākāśa* (space), in *śāntātīta kalā*. *Naiva kiṁcid dhāmāsti*, it has not some particular place where one reaches and gets liberated from repeated births and deaths.

Na cāpi gamanamanyatra, for *mokṣa*, for attaining *mokṣa*, you have not to tread from the state where you are already existing in the field of *māyā*. You are existing in the field of *māyā* and you have to get elevated by and by, by and by, by *abhyasa*[140]. But you

140 Contemplative practice.

have not to tread. There is no journey to be covered. The starting point of the journey is the ending point of the journey!

PS DVD 3 (00:54:25)

भिन्नाज्ञानग्रन्थि-
गतसंदेहः पराकृतभ्रान्तिः ।
प्रक्षीणपुण्यपापो
विग्रहयोगेऽप्यसौ मुक्तः ॥६१॥

bhinnājñāna-granthir-
gata-saṁdehaḥ parākṛta-bhrāntiḥ /
prakṣīṇa-puṇya-pāpo
vigraha-yoge'py-asau muktaḥ //61//

Bhinnājñāna granthir, the person who has [*bhinna*] *ājñāna granthi*, who has cut all the bindings of ignorance–all the bindings of ignorance which are three kinds of ignorance: *āṇavamala*, *mayīyamala*, and *kārmamala*[141]–who has discarded this threefold ignorance, *gata-saṁdehaḥ*, who has crossed all the doubts in achievement, . . .

Because, what is to be achieved is already achieved. You have not to put effort for Its achievement. If you put effort for Its achievement, you won't achieve It. You have not to put effort for Its achievement. You have to see if It is achieved or not achieved. If It is not achieved, It will never be achieved! If It is achieved, It will never be not-achieved! Understand? This is the truth existing behind it. He who says, "I am a *murkha*", he will remain always a *murkha*, he will remain always a duffer. He who says, "I am Lord Śiva", he is always Lord Śiva.

. . . *prakṣīṇa puṇya pāpa*, where he has absolutely come out from the circles of good deeds and bad deeds and its fruit also–its bearing fruit also, he has come out from that binding; he has no binding whatsoever like this–*vigrahayoga api*, although he is walking, and he has got toothache also, and calcium deficiency, and he uses that [medicine] bottle prescribed by doctor Jonathan

141 For an explanation of the *malas*, see Appendix A-3.

[laughter], still he is *mukta* (liberated), although he is dragging this body like human beings.

PS DVD 3 (00:57:15)

अग्न्यभिदग्धं बीजं
　　यथा प्ररोहासमर्थतामेति ।
ज्ञानाग्निदग्धमेवं
　　कर्म न जन्मप्रदं भवति ॥६२॥

agny-abhidagdhaṁ bījaṁ
　　yathā prarohāsamarthatām-eti /
jñānāgni-dagdham-evaṁ
　　karma na janma-pradaṁ bhavati //62//

Agnyabhidagdhaṁ bījaṁ–bījaṁ means "seed"; he goes again to that [analogy of the] seed–*agnyabhidagdhaṁ*, when on fire it will be baked, any seed, *yathā prarohāsamarthatām*, if it is sown in spring time, [in] good time, when there is good soil, everything, and he puts water also from time to time, *prarohāsamarthatāmeti*, it does not produce a sprout [Swamiji sings these last few words].

DENISE: Oh [laughs]!

SWAMIJI: [laughs] Why? What do you say?

DENISE: It was good.

SWAMIJI: *Jñānāgnidagdhamevaṁ karma na janma pradaṁ bhavati*, in the same way, all your activities, whatever you do–good, bad, and crush people, cheat people, give bad names to everybody, and do blunders, whatever you do–*jñāna agni dagdhamevaṁ karma*, if you put that in the fire of Parabhairava knowledge–whatever action you do; good and bad and wretched and rascal actions–*na janma pradaṁ bhavati*, it will just direct you to the Parabhairava state and you won't be caught in the pangs of repeated births and deaths again by those brutal actions also–if once, by the grace of God, by *tīvra śaktipāta*, you will fire them with the knowledge of Parabhairava.

PS DVD 3 (00:59:25)

परिमितबुद्धित्वेन हि
कर्मोचितभाविदेहभावनया ।
संकुचिता चितिरेतद्-
देहध्वंसे तथा भवति ॥६३॥

parimita-buddhitvena hi
karmocita-bhāvi-deha bhāvanayā[142] /
saṁkucitā citir-etad-
deha-dhvaṁse tathā bhavati //*63*//

On the contrary, *parimita buddhitvena*, when you are shrunk, always shrunk, you do *abhyāsa* [and think], "I want to realize God. I can't realize God. I want to see God!"–*parimita buddhitvena hi karmocita-bhāvi-deha-bhāvanayā*. *Saṁkucitā citiretad*, he has always carried his consciousness, shrunken consciousness, with him. He is always crying, "I have not achieved anything! I have not achieved anything! O master, when shall I achieve anything?" *Deha-dhvaṁse tathā bhavati*, when he dies, he dies also in the same manner, and he is caught by repeated births and deaths again. It is his . . .

DENISE: His own doing?

SWAMIJI: . . . it is his own thinking. Whatever you think, that gets it's shape, [it comes] true. If you think, "I am Parabhairava", it will get its shape–true. If you think, "I am not. I am trodden. I am a fool. I am worth nothing", [then] you are worth nothing.

END Paramārthasara DVD 3 (01:01:07)

142 Whilst reciting this verse, Swamiji chants "*samiraṇayā*" instead of "*bhāvanayā*". Swamiji does not, however, note this change in the original text from which he was reading. [*Editor's note*]

DVD Four

yadi punaramalaṁ . . .

On the contrary now. He [explains] these opposite sections. These are two opposite posts. They are conducting side-by-side, because the conducting of these two posts is not different from each other. It is one; it is one conducting. But the first is situated in Parabhairava and the other is situated in repeated births and deaths.

Now, this is the first-class being:

PS DVD 4 (00:00:49)

यदि पुनरमलं बोधं
सर्वसमुत्तीर्णबोद्धृकर्तृमयम् ।
विततमनस्तमितोदित-
भारूपं सत्यसंकल्पम् ॥६४॥
दिक्कालकलनविकलं
ध्रुवमव्ययमीश्वरं सुपरिपूर्णम् ।
बहुतरशक्तिव्रात-
प्रलयोदयविरचनैककर्तारम् ॥६५॥
सृष्ट्यादिविधिसुवेधस-
मात्मानं शिवमयं विबुध्येत ।

yadi punar-amalaṁ bodhaṁ
sarva-samuttīrṇa-boddhṛ-kartṛ-mayam /
vitatam-anastamitodita-
bhārūpaṁ satya-saṁkalpam //64//

dik-kāla-kalana-vikalaṁ
dhruvam-avyayam-īśvaraṁ suparipūrṇam /
bahutara-śakti-vrāta-
pralayodaya-viracanaika-kartāram //65//
sṛṣṭy-ādi-vidhi-suvedhasam-
ātmānaṁ śivam-ayaṁ vibuddhyeta /

Yadi punar amalaṁ, if *punar*[143], by the *tīvra-tīvra śaktipāta* of Parabhairava, *ātmānaṁ*, one feels his own Self . . .

In which way?

. . . *amalaṁ bodham*, that I am absolutely the purest crystal, like pure; *sarva samuttīrṇa boddhṛ-kartṛ-mayam*, I have got all power of knowledge and all power of doing, topmost, I possess that knowledge; *vitatam*, I am *vitatam,* everywhere seen, I am everywhere existing; *anastamitodita bhārūpa*, and my *prakāśa*, my light, it is [everlasting] light, I possess that light; *satya saṁkalpam*, and whatever I think, that comes true.

[Not] that [it] *comes* true; that *is* true, that *is* there! If I say, "This house is a rock", it will become a rock. [If I say], "This house is nothing, this is *bakwas* (nonsense)", and it becomes *bakwas*. [If I say], "There are those sheep–'*baaaaaah*'–in place of this house", [that comes true]. They are doing, '*baaaaah*'. Whatever you think, it will become that. If you think, "It is my Self", [you] will become Bhairava; [you] will be crystal-like, throwing light all around. And that is *satya saṁkalpa*, he thinks and that becomes [true].

Tat sṛṣṭā tadevāna praveśa, whatever he creates, he becomes that.

Dik kāla kalana vikalaṁ. Dik kāla kalanaṁ, he is away from the limitation of space (*dik*), *kāla* (limitation of time), *akala* (the limitation of formation). He is away from these three things: space, time, and formation. *Vikalaṁ* means, the negation of, the non-existence of, these three.

Dhruvam means eternal; *avyayam*, non-ending; *īśvaraṁ*, powerful behavior and handler of this whole universe; *supari pūrṇam*, and full, always full, never is emptied from his glamour.

He gives more qualifications of this being:

Bahutara-śakti-vrata pralayodaya-viracanaika-kartāram.

143 On the contrary.

Bahutara śakti vrata, and there are so many numberless energies, *śakti-cakra*, of Parabhairava. He creates those energies, and he maintains those energies, and he . . .

DENISE: Destroys?

SWAMIJI: No.

. . . he closes the drama of the energies. There is no energy left.

JOHN: Withdraws?

SWAMIJI: Withdraws. Withdraws into nowhere. The energies are nowhere seen.

Energies are seen, everywhere. He is the creator (he is the producer), and he is protecting those energies, and he is withdrawing those energies, i.e., [when] the energies are not seen at all.

Sṛṣṭyādividhisuvedhasam. Sṛṣṭi ādi vidhi suvedhasam, he creates this world, he protects this world . . . . he creates this world as Brahma, he protects this world as Viṣṇu, he destroys this world as Rūdra, he conceals this world as Īśvara, and he reveals this world as Sadāśiva, Śiva.

If he, by his own will and power of *tīvra-tīvra śaktipāta*, *vibuddhyeta*, if by his own grace, he comes to its understanding, . . .

कथमिव संसारी स्याद्
वितातस्य कुतः क्व वा सरणम् ॥६६॥

katham-iva saṁsārī syād
vitatasya kutaḥ kva vā saraṇam //66b//
[not recited in full]

. . . how can he be called an individual, trodden, and a poor fellow who is created poor, pitied–*katham*, how? He will never get this position afterwards.

Vitatasya, he has become *vitata* (*vitata* means "he is expanded in all ways"). *Vitatasya kutaḥ kva vā saraṇam*, where will he go? Wherever he goes, if it is down, that is up; if it is up, that is down. Wherever he goes, up and down is just a dream, just a drama for him.

PS DVD 4 (00:08:00)

इति युक्तिभिरपि सिद्धं
यत्कर्म ज्ञानिनो न सफलं तत्
न ममेदमपि तु तस्ये-
ति दार्ढ्यतो नहि फलं लोके ॥६७॥

iti yuktibhir-api siddhaṁ
yat-karma jñānino na saphalaṁ tat
na mamedam-api tu tasye-
ti dārḍhyato nahi phalaṁ loke //67//

In the same way–in these ways which I have [explained] here–*yat karma siddhaṁ*, whatever action he does, *jñāninā*, he who is elevated, *na saphalaṁ tat*, he does not produce any fruit, because he says, after doing each and every fraud-full action in this world, he believes, "I have done nothing. These are the organs of the body which do." And there are five [causes], those which are responsible [for every action], which you have been explained in the commentary of the *Bhagavad Gītā*: "*pañcaite tasya hetavaḥ*", five are responsible, five great things.[144]

---

144 ". . . it is explained that there are five great actors in this world, who are adjusted in each and every action, whatever you do. The first great actor is *adhiṣṭāna*, [the] basis, on which base [all] action is done. The base is just the state of Lord Śiva. Action is done in the basis of Lord Śiva. That is the chief actor, chief player. Without the basis, nothing will be done. When there is not the state of Lord Śiva, no action will take place. *Tathā kartā*, now that individual actor is the second, second player. *Karaṇaṁ ca pṛthagvidham*, and the organic field, the gathering of organs. The gathering of organs is the third substance of action. Because you [can't] do any action without organs, [without] either the hand or nose or tongue or eye–any action. So these gathering of the organs is the third active player. *Vividhā ca pṛthakceṣṭā*, and ambitions, various ambitions in your mind, this is the forth actor. And *daivam-evātra*, the fifth is *prārabdha* [*karma*]. *Daivam*, destiny is the fifth action, the fifth actor." Swami Lakshmanjoo, *Bhagavad Gītā* audio, USF archive. See also *Bhagavad Gītā–In the Light of Kashmir Shaivism*, 18.13-15.

PS DVD 4 (00:09:35)

इत्थं सकलविकल्पान्
प्रतिबुद्धो भावनासमीरणतः ।
आत्मज्योतिषि दीप्ते
जुह्वज्ज्योतिर्मयो भवति ॥६८॥

ittham sakala-vikalpān
pratibuddho bhāvanā-samīraṇataḥ /
ātma-jyotiṣi dīpte
juhvaj-jyotir-mayo bhavati //68//

In this way, *sakala vikalpān*, in this way, *prati buddha*, he who is elevated, and who is elevated and who is installed by his own *śaktipāta* (grace), installed in the supreme knowledge of Parabhairava, *bhāvanā samīraṇataḥ*, he creates that *bhāvana*, the perception, that, "I am Maheśvara! I am Parabhairava! I am the source of each and every being! And each and every being is my own manifestation!"

Ātma jyotiṣi dīpte. All these *vikalpas*[145], limited and unlimited, he [burns] in *ātma jyotiṣa dipte*, which are elevated [in] his own fire of God consciousness.[146] *Jyotirmayo bhavati,* he is only shining; he becomes a being of light, tremendous light. And his way of behavior in life, he explains again:

PS DVD 4 (00:11:38)

अश्नन् यद्वा तद्वा
संवीतो येन केनचिच्छान्तः ।
यत्र क्वचन निवासी
विमुच्यते सर्वभूतात्मा ॥६९॥

145 Varieties of thoughts, impressions.

146 "When all these [*kalpanāḥ*] are offered in the fire of Lord Bhairava, [they] become just one with *chidagniḥ*, [the fire of consciousness], and nothing other than That." (Swami Lakshmanjoo's handwritten notes)

aśnan yadvā tadvā
samvīto yena kenacic-chāntaḥ /
yatra kvacana nivāsī
vimucyate sarva-bhūtātmā //69//

Aśnan yadvā tadvā, he eats . . . whatever comes in front of him, he eats that. *Samvīto yena kenacit*, he covers his body [with] whatever, just like I told you.[147] *Sānta*, he is always peaceful. *Yatra kvacana nivāsī*, he does not mind to remain particularly in a brahmin's house. He does not get afraid of remaining in a butcher's house and all [those] who are an outcast, e.g., he who eats dogs' flesh. *Vimucyate sarvabhūtātmā*, he is always *jīvan mukta*[148] because he is the same in each and every respect. Nothing will affect him.[149]

अनियतफलभक्ष्यभोज्यपेयं
विधिपरिणामविभक्तदेशकालम् ।
हृदयसुखमसेवितं कदर्यै-
र्व्रतमिदमाजगरं शुचिश्चरामि ॥

aniyata-phala-bhakṣya-bhojya-peyaṁ
vidhi-pariṇāma-vibhakta-deśa-kālam /
hṛdaya-sukhama-sevitaṁ kadaryair
vratam-idam-ājagaraṁ śuciścarāmi //[150]

Aniyata phala bhakṣya bhojya peyaṁ. Whose by *bhojya* and *peya*, . . .

Bhakṣya means eatable things, what is to be eaten. *Bhojya* means what is to be crushed with the teeth. For instance, *channa* (chickpeas), it is *bhojya*, you have to [chew] it. *Peyam* is milk, or

147 Referring to verse 15.
148 Liberated while embodied.
149 "With what[ever] his body is covered, or with whom he eats, or on what[ever] he sleeps–a divine bed or on rocks–God considers that being as divine Bhairava." (Swami Lakshmanjoo's handwritten notes)
150 Yogarāja's commentary.

virapāṇa. That is *peyam*. You know *virapāṇa*? Heroic water[151]. That is *peyam*. And this Coca-Cola and Thumbs-Up, it is *virapāṇa*, it is called *peya*. *Bhojya* means [that which] is to be [chewed].

. . . *vidhi pariṇāma vibhakta deśa kālam*, according to the *vidhi* (*vidhi* means the things which are happening according to the creation of *prakṛti* and his *māyā śakti*), whatever comes in front of him, *hṛdaya sukham asevitaṁ kadaryair*; *hṛdaya sukham*, he is absolutely peacefully situated in his heart of Parabhairava, which is *kadaryair asevitaṁ* . . .

> *Kadaryair*, those who are shrunken, those are afraid from this kind of differentiatedness, they will never leave [expensive] clothes and cover their bodies with tart[152]. Their [expensive] clothes also, they will keep in a trunk. Those are *kadaryais*[153].

. . . and in that *hṛdaya sukha*[154], which [is] maintained by Parabhairava, sometimes [he wears a] *pashmina*[155] and sometimes a tart. And his *pashmina* he throws on the roadside [and says], "What is a *pashmina*? A tart is also the same thing. *Vratam idamājagaraṁ śuciścarāmi*, this *vratam*, this maintenance of my being, which is the purest thing, I tread on that *vrata*. This is my behavior. This is the real behavior of my being Bhairava."

PS DVD 4 (00:16:42)

हयमेधशतसहस्रा-
ण्यपि, कुरुते ब्रह्मघातलक्षाणि ।

151 Liquor.
152 Jute.
153 The person established in the Parabhairava state abstains (*asevita*) from such miserly (*kadarya*) conduct. [*Editor's note*]
154 Peaceful heart.
155 The finest type of Kashmir wool.

परमार्थविन्न पुण्यै-
 र्न च पापैः स्पृश्यते विमलः ॥७०॥

haya-medha-śata sahasrā-
ṇyapi, kurute brahma-ghāta-lakṣāṇi /
paramārtha-vinna puṇyair
na ca pāpaiḥ spṛśyate vimalaḥ //70//

Haya-medha-śata sahasrāṇyapi. If he conducts *aśvamedha*[156], *śata sahasrāṇi*, one *lakh* (100,000) of *aśvamedha*, one *lakh* times of *aśvamedha yajñā*s, *kurute brahmaghāta lakhsāṇi*, or he does *brahmaghāta lakhsāni*, he kills and slaughters at least 100,000 *lakhs* of people, he slaughters and cuts the head of those [people],[157] *paramārthavinna puṇyair na ca pāpaiḥ spṛśyate vimalam*, he is *vimala*, he is pure, he is the pure element, he is not caught by those crimes, neither is he caught by . . . what?

JOHN: Those crimes.

SWAMIJI: . . . those kinds of virtuous deeds. He is above virtuous deeds and tremendous deeds.[158]

haya-medha-śata sahasrā-
ṇyapi, kurute brahma-ghāta-lakṣāṇi /
paramārtha-vinna puṇyair
na ca pāpaiḥ spṛśyate vimalaḥ //70//
[repeated]

[Swamiji sings without words]

Bas. I don't know what to do with others.

---

156 *Aśvamedha yajñā* was an ancient Vedic ritual in which horses were sacrificed.

157 "Highly good activities or highly bad sinful deeds." (Swami Lakshmanjoo's handwritten notes)

158 "As he is the purest divine being." Ibid.

PS DVD 4 (00:18:57)

मदहर्षकोपमन्मथ-
विषादभयलोभमोहपरिवर्जी ।
निःस्तोत्रवषट्कारो
जड इव विचरेदवादमतिः ॥७१॥

mada-harṣa-kopa-manmatha-
viṣāda-bhaya-lobha-moha-parivarjī /
niḥstotra-vaṣaṭ-kāro
jaḍa iva vicared-avāda-matiḥ //71//

evaṁ vidhasya jñānino niyatacaryāṁ parāmṛśannāha[159]

That [person] who has attained the state of Parabhairava, how he behaves in the *śeṣa vṛtti*, in the remaining period of his livelihood? What is his behavior that he conducts in the remaining portion of his life? Because he has achieved what was to be achieved, but still he must have some engagement. What is his engagement?

Mada is the first–number one. *Mada*–you put that?

JOHN: Yes, sir.

SWAMIJI: *Mada* means *deha pramātṛtā abhimānaḥ*. This is . . . I have to take the commentary of Yogarāja also at the same time.

1. *Mada* is *deha pramātṛtā abhimānaḥ*, that, "I am this body". This is *mada*, this is ego. This *parivrajī*[160], he discards this. He has not this ego that, "I am the body".

2. *Harṣa*. *Harṣa* means "excitement". Excitement does not mean excitement. Excitement means, *alabadhasya lābhāt pramodaḥ*, *harṣa* means whatever was not achieved by him by doing some effort, . . .

[Usually], when one achieves [some fruit from his effort], he gets some excitement. But it is the reverse, his behavior is the reverse.

---

159 Yogarāja's commentary.
160 To wander about as a religious mendicant.

. . . if he has put exertion for achieving something, if he has achieved, he does not get excitement. If he does not achieve, he also does not get grief. He remains the same in both conditions. This is the difference in his behavior of his *śeṣa vṛtti* (*śeṣa* [*vṛtti*] means "in the remaining period of his life"). *Harṣa* is the second.

3. And *kopaḥ*. *Kopa* means *krodha*, wrath. But he discards that wrath. There is no sign of wrath at all in him. That is the third sign.

4. Fourth is *manmathaḥ*. *Manmatha* means the desire for sex. The desire for sex is called *manmatha*. *Manmatha* is the fourth.

5. *Viṣādaḥ* is the fifth. *Viṣādaḥ* means, when you are overgrieved . . .

Manmatha, he has no *manmatha*, he has no desire for sex. He has lost the desire for sex altogether because he has undergone another "super-sex".[161]

Viṣādaḥ. *Viṣādaḥ* means "grief". There is an absence of grief in him, whereas others have grief. What is *viṣāda*? *Iṣṭaviyogāt mūḍhatvam*; *iṣṭaviyogāt*, [one] who is your dear and very beloved, and [after] he has passed away, or she has passed away, you remain gloomy in the remaining period of your life. He does not do that. He remains the same. If his very well-behaved wife passes away, still he remains the same. He says, "This is the way of the world. Why should I bother?"

6. *Bhayaṁ*. And threat; he has no threat, [no] threat from anybody, [no] threat from an enemy. Neither he has threat from an enemy nor [from] someone else. He is without threat. Threat he does not allow in his mind.

Threat is which number?

JOHN: Seven.

SWAMIJI: No, threat is eighth.

JOHN: What is before threat?

SWAMIJI: Yes, it is seventh, it is seventh.

Siṁhavyāghrādervā daraḥ, or threat is, e.g., he is afraid of a

---

161 "It is not actually sexual pleasure. It is the source of sexual pleasure, because by sexual pleasure you are trodden down. And this sexual delight (I would not call it "sexual pleasure"; it is sexual delight), this is sex between Lord Śiva and Pārvatī there. So this will make you rise. You will never fall from this delight of super-sex." Swami Lakshmanjoo, *Interviews*, USF archive.

tiger or a lion. [But] he is never afraid of a lion. It can scratch and behave [towards] him just in a friendly [manner] and he will put his arms and embrace it. [The beast] won't do anything to him. It is his behavior in the remaining period of life.[162]

7. *Lobhaḥ. Lobhaḥ* means attachment.

Which is the number?

JOHN: That's number seven.[163]

SWAMIJI: *Lobha* means *kārpaṇyaṁ. Kārpaṇyaṁ* means, he is squeezed, his nerves are squeezed, e.g., because he likes Viresh, he won't like Oṁ Prakāśa[164]. You won't like Oṁ Prakāśa, you will like Viresh. Would you [not]? Never! But he does not behave like that. It seems, to him, one and the same thing.

8. And *moha. Moha* is now the eighth. *Moha* is *būteṣu ātmātmīyabhāvaḥ*, e.g., "This is mine and this is not mine."

etān deha-saṁskārapratyavamarśān madhye samāyātānapi[165]

These, if they come to him, he discards them and says, "*Sarvaṁ brahmāsmi*, it is the drama of Parabhairava. Why should I worry about these rules and regulations?"

So,

निःस्तोत्रवषड्कारो
जड इव विचरेदवादमतिः ॥७१॥

niḥstotra-vaṣaṭ-kāro
jaḍa iva vicared-avāda-matiḥ //71//
[repeated]

162 Viz., *ahiṁsāpratiṣṭhāyāṁ tatsannidhau vairatyāgaḥ* // (*Yoga Sūtras*, "Sādhanā Pāda", 35). "No power on earth can make two mutual enemies enter into combat in the presence of he, who being established in subtle non-violence, does not harm anyone." Swami Lakshmanjoo, *Practice and Discipline*, USF archive.

163 Wherever the numbers are incorrect in the recording, they have been corrected in the transcript. [*Editors note*]

164 Oṁ Prakāśa was Swamiji's cook.

165 Yogarāja's commentary.

9. *Niḥstotravaṣaṭkāra*. He does not get dependent to *stotravaṣaṭkāra*, i.e., who[ever] behaves [towards] him with reverence or who does not behave [towards] him with reverence, who hates him. *Niḥstotravaṣaṭkāra*, he has the same feeling for both these classes–[those] who behave [towards] him in a good sense or in a bad sense.

Jaḍa iva vicaredavādamatiḥ, he roams, he is seen everywhere in the world, walking and behaving and talking, but inside he is untouched by all these two things, opposite two things.

For this, Nilakāntha *brahmacarī* . . .

[Do] you know Nilakāntha brahmacarī?

GEORGE: He went to Rishikesh.

DENISE: Yes.

SWAMIJI: . . . he also, when he heard this, he also said, "From the Vedānta point of view, Śaṅkarācharya had also placed this *śloka*. The same meaning comes out from that [verse]:

एतावदेव खलुलिंगम् अलिंग-मूर्त्तेः
संशान्त-संस्रतिचिर-भ्रमनिर्वृत्तेस्य ।
तज्ञस्य यद्-मदनकोपविशादमोह-
लोभापदामनुदिनं निपुणतनुत्वम् ॥

etāvadeva khalu-liṅgam aliṅgamūrtteḥ
saṁśānta-saṁsraticira-bhrama-nirvṛttesya /
tajñasya yad-madana-kopa-viśāda-moha-
lobhāpadāmanudinaṁ nipuṇatanutvam / /[166]

Etāvadeva khaluliṅgam aliṅga mūrtteḥ. This is the main sign in the behavior of Parabhairava, [of one] who is situated in the state of Parabhairava: *aliṅga mūrtteḥ*, he has no sign of being a saint. He is not behaving saintly, he is not behaving not-saintly.

Saṁśānta saṁsraticira bhrama nirvṛttesya. And *saṁsrati*, the

---

166 This verse, handwritten by Swamiji, is a slight variation from Mokṣopāya 6.130.19 of the Yoga Vasiṣṭha. Note: This verse does not appear in the text of the *Paramārthasāra*.

threat of being entangled in repeated births and deaths, this threat he has absolutely cent-per-cent[167] negation of this threat. This threat is not seen in his being. And this is the greatest sign in him that is seen after he realizes the state of Parabhairava.

Madanakopaviśādamoha lobhāpadāmanudinaṁ nipuṇatanutvam. These nine things, you see [in] him that these nine things [are] decaying one after another, one after another, and, in the end, they are not seen at all in him. They go only in nothingness, zero. They become zero, i.e., these nine behaviors.

Because it was Vedānta[168], so they say that they become zero in the end. But the Shaivite does not understand that. The Shaivite thinks that they are zero altogether, there. But the Vedāntists say that they become zero when he leaves his body. That is the difference between Vedānta and Shaivism. Otherwise, all *śāstras*[169] go to that state.

JOHN: So, those Vedāntins don't believe in this state of Parabhairava.

SWAMIJI: No, they don't believe in that.

GEORGE: Because they are always negating qualities.

SWAMIJI: Qualities, yes. They say these qualities end only at the time of death, not in his lifetime.

PS DVD 4 (00:32:57)

मदहर्षप्रभृतिरयं
वर्गः प्रभवति विभेदसंमोहात् ।
अद्वैतात्मविबोध-
स्तेन कथं स्पृश्यतां नाम ॥७२॥

167 One hundred percent.

168 The original *Paramārthasāra* of Patañjali is written from the point of view of Vedānta. Abhinavagupta's recension of the text gives it a "whitewash of Shaivism". See also commentary on verses 2 and 3.

169 Scriptures.

mada-harṣa-prabhṛtir-ayaṁ
vargaḥ prabhavati vibheda-saṁmohāt /
advaitātma-vibodhas-
tena kathaṁ spṛśyatāṁ nāma //72//

Mada-harṣa-prabhṛtir-ayaṁ vargaḥ. This nine-fold behavior, *prabhavati vibheda-saṁmohāt*, by differentiated perception, it rises–this nine-fold class. But, *advaita ātma vibodha*, one who is *advaita ātma vibodha*, one who is absolutely united in the Parabhairava state, *tena kathaṁ spṛśyatāṁ nāma*, how this will . . . ? This [nine-fold behavior] has no guts to remain in his intellectual field. It has no guts.[170]

PS DVD 4 (00:34:06)

स्तुत्यं वा होतव्यं
नास्ति व्यतिरिक्तमस्य किंचन च ।
स्तोत्रादिना स तुष्येन्
मुक्तस्तन्निर्नमस्कृतिवषट्कः ॥७३॥

stutyaṁ vā hotavyaṁ
nāsti vyatiriktam-asya kiṁcana ca /
stotrādinā sa tuṣyen
muktas-tan-nirnamaskṛti-vaṣaṭkaḥ //73//

Stutya hotavya, nāsti vyatiriktam. He does not believe in other gods, he does not believe himself as the worshiper of gods. This behavior is not found in his perception. *Stotrādinā tuṣyet*, so, by *stotrās* (hymns) or *namskāras* (prostrations), he does not get moved. You may behave [towards] him in a godly way, you may behave [towards] him brutely, [but] he is the same. He is out of this circle.

This is the seventy-third, ending.

---

170 "They also are not other than what he has attained." (Swami Lakshmanjoo's handwritten notes)

PS DVD 4 (00:35:07)

षड्त्रिंशत्तत्त्वभृतं
विग्रहरचनागवाक्षपरिपूर्णम् ।
निजमन्यदथ शरीरं
घटादि वा तस्य देवगृहम् ॥७४॥

ṣaṭ-triṁśat-tattva-bhṛtaṁ
vigraha-racanā-gavākṣa-paripūrṇam /
nija-manya-datha śarīraṁ
ghaṭādi vā tasya devagṛham / /74/ /

Saṭtriṁśat tattva bhṛtaṁ, the body, which is conducted with the thirty-six elements, this body, the human body, *vigraha racanāgavākṣa paripūrṇam*, this body is just like the *devagṛha* (*devagṛha* means, this is a temple, a temple of Parabhairava), this body is the temple of Parabhairava laid out in this world. *Vigraha racanāgavākṣa paripūrṇam*, and it has got doors and windows and everything. That is, it has got nine doors, nine openings–these eyes, nostrils, etc. It has come in . . .

GEORGE: *Navarandhragāḥ*.

SWAMIJI: *Navarandhra*[171].

---

171 This word, which means "nine openings", appears in the following hymn dedicated to Amṛteśvara, the Lord of nectar:

dvāreśā navarandhragāḥ hṛidayago-vāstur gaṇeśo mahān
śabdādyā guruvaḥ samīradaśakaṁ tvādhāra śaktyātmakam ।
ciddevo 'tha vimarśa śakti sahitaḥ ṣāḍguṇyam aṅgāvalir
lokeśāḥ karaṇāni yasya mahimā taṁ netranāthaṁ stumaḥ । ।

"I bow to that Netranātha, Amṛteśvara, who is fond of His nectar producing third eye, and in whose glamorous body the nine openings are nine doorkeepers which are the nine incarnations of Gaṇeśa (Dvāreśā); whose heart is Gaṇeśa, His son, the director of the one hundred Vāstu Devatā; whose five sensations are the five classes of Masters; whose *mūladhāra cakra* consists of the ten layers of *vāyu* (air) which fill the universe; who is the Lord of Consciousness always united with His energy of consciousness; whose six limbs are His six universal

Nijamanyadatha śarīraṁ, his body, or another's body, *ghaṭādi vā*, or the objective world, *tasya devagṛham*, for him, it is all a collection of temples, the temples of Parabhairava. This pot is also the temple of Parabhairava. This machinery is also the temple of Parabhairava. Because Parabhairava comes out of it, in one way or in another. Or this [body] is the temple of Parabhairava, and inside the heart is the temple of Parabhairava. Everywhere you will find Parabhairava. And this whole universal world, one hundred and eighteen worlds, is the temple of Parabhairava. And there, in that temple of Parabhairava, these temples . . .

How many temples are there?

Numberless temples!

And this is also a temple, this is also a temple, this is also a temple.[172] And this whole is also a temple. The part is also a temple. The part is the whole and the whole is the part. You can't find any distinction between the part and the whole.

Do you understand?

And there, . . .

PS DVD 4 (00:37:47)

तत्र च परमात्ममहा-
भैरवशिवदेवतां स्वशक्तियुताम् ।
आत्मामर्शनविमल-
द्रव्यैः परिपूजयन्नास्ते ॥७५॥

tatra ca paramātma-mahā-
bhairava-śiva-devatāṁ sva-śakti-yutām /
ātmāmarśana-vimala-
dravyaiḥ paripūjayannāste //75//

---

attributes (all-knowingness, complete fullness, eternal knowledge, absolute freedom, inexhaustible energy, and infinite energies); and whose ten internal organs are the ten protectors of this world protecting it from all ten sides." *Sacred Verses for Worship*, Swami Lakshmanjoo, page 20.

172 Swamiji gestures to indicate that each person in the room is also a temple of Parabhairava.

. . . in that body (it is one body), . . .*
How many bodies?
Numberless!

JOHN: Numberless parts.

SWAMIJI: Numberless bodies!

JOHN: Bodies?

SWAMIJI: Yes, numberless bodies of Parabhairava–temples, the temples of Parabhairava. I told you, this whole universe is filled with temples.

JOHN: But there is one body of Parabhairava.

SWAMIJI: In fact, it is one body. This body is one, and this body is millions, a million temples!

JOHN: So this verse, this "*dvāreśā*", this is adoration to this universal body.

SWAMIJI: Yes, that universal body. It is not *navarandhragāḥ* (nine openings) only in the human body. *Navarandhras* are everywhere found.

*. . . and there, *tatra*, in the temple of one's own body, *tatra ca paramātma mahābhairava śiva devatāṁ*, there you will find *paramātma mahā bhairava devatā svaśaktiyutām*, [the One] who has got all five energies (*cit śakti*, *ānanda śakti*, *icchā śakti*, *jñāna śakti*, and *kriyā śakti*). It is filled with all these five energies and their offshoots, which are numberless offshoots of energies. It is filled with that.

And there, *ātma āmarśana vimala dravyaiḥ*, sometimes he takes toast and puts butter on it, or jam on it. This is his *pūja*. He does, he operates, the *pūja* of Parabhairava. And this is also Parabhairava, this is also Parabhairava with which you operate, with which you worship your body [Swamiji demonstrates the act of eating].

And Viresh says, "No, I want curds! I don't want at all this nonsense *makan* (butter). I don't like this butter. I like curds, thick curds." Some say, "I want thin curds". In the same way, it is one and the same thing. And curds are also Parabhairava, and the one who is fed with curds is Parabhairava, and by which he feeds the curds, by his hands, is Parabhairava. There is no way out from Parabhairava. Parabhairava is everywhere.

Tatra, everywhere, is *paramātma mahābhairava devatā sva-śaktiyutām*, and he is with the embodiment of His full energies.

Ātma āmarśana vimala dravyaiḥ paripūja, and he is doing his *pūja*, day and night. In the night, he does his *pūja* [by] "*zzzzz, zzzzz*" [Swamiji imitates the sound of snoring]. This is his *pūja*. This is *pūja*. He is nowhere there.

Don't you understand what I mean?

JOHN: Everything you do is *pūja* to the Lord, is it? When you go to bathroom, you are also doing *pūja*.

SWAMIJI: This is the best *pūja*! Bathroom is, on the contrary, it is the best *pūja*, it is the purest *pūja*.

When *pūja* is ending, then there must be some behavior in conducting *havan*[173] also. What is *havan* for this Parabhairava? How he offers this mutual *havan*?

JOHN: *Havan* means *yajñā*?

SWAMIJI: *Yajñā* (sacrifice).

PS DVD 4 (00:41:57)

बहिरन्तरपरिकल्पन-
भेदमहाबीजनिचयमर्पयतः ।
तस्यातिदीप्तसंवि-
ज्वलने यत्नाद्विना भवति होमः ॥७६॥

bahir-antara-parikalpana-
bheda-mahā-bīja-nicayam-arpayataḥ /
tasyāti-dīpta-saṁvit-
jvalane yatnād-vinā bhavati homaḥ //76//

Bahir antara parikalpana bheda mahā bīja nicayamarpa-yataḥ. Mahā bīja means that *sāmagrī*[174]. What is that *sāmagrī*? *Sāmagrī* is Parabhairava. Parabhairava is to be offered in the fire of Parabhairava. In the fire of Parabhairava, you have to offer Parabhairava, by the hands of Parabhairava, by the hands

173 The act of offering oblations in a fire.

174 *Sāmagrī* is a traditional mixture of natural and sanctified ingredients that are used as offerings in a *havan* (*yajñā*) ceremony.

which are Parabhairava, and [into the] fire which is Parabhairava[175]–*bheda mahā bīja nicayamarpayataḥ*.

Tasyāti dīpta saṁvit jvalane. This is *saṁvit jvalane*, the fire of God consciousness is burning everywhere. *Yat na ādvinā bhavati homaḥ*, without doing effort for *havan*, he [conducts] *havan*, he has done *havan*, he is always doing *havan*.

This is also *havan* [Swamiji scratches himself]. This is *havan*, this is *havan*. He has done this *havan* in Parabhairava. Because, this was the first thing–this feeling [of an itch]–and then, when you are satisfied [after scratching it], that is the end of *havan*. The *havan* is conducted.

There is another *havan* now. Another *havan* is now a corn on the foot. You [place] that bandage on it, and this is *havan*.

He says, "*Havan* is everything!"

JOHN: So what is *havan* then? How does it differ from *pūja*?

SWAMIJI: There is no difference. *Pūja* is also the same. *Havan* is also the same. Whatever you think. Devil is also the same. Everything is *havan*. *Havan* is everything. *Pūja* is everything.

JOHN: What is the real difference between *havan* and *pūja*? Is there a difference between [them]?

SWAMIJI: There is no difference. There is no difference. There is no "between". Everything is *havan*, everything is *pūja*, everything is brutality, everything is bad names–everything.[176] That is what he says here in this *śloka*, seventy-six.

> *bahir-antara-parikalpana-*
> *bheda-mahā-bīja-nicayam-arpayataḥ* /
> *tasyāti-dīpta-saṁvit-*
> *jvalane yatnād-vinā bhavati homaḥ* //76//
> [repeated]

Without *homa* (fire ceremony), he offers. He has conducted *homa* without doing *homa*. Without doing *pūja*, he has conducted *pūja* also. Without doing anything, he has done that thing.

---

175 See *Bhagavad Gītā–In the Light of Kashmir Shaivism*, 4.24.

176 That is, every act, even brutality or the use of harsh words, is an act of worship for one who is established in the state of Parabhairava, the state of universal God consciousness. [*Editor's note*]

What is *dhyāna*[177] for him? "*Dhyāna* also", Abhinavagupta says, "*dhyāna* also is the same way." *Dhyāna* is not only *dhyāna* of God consciousness (*cit śakti*, *ānanda śakti*, *icchā śakti*, *jñāna śakti*, and *kriyā śakti*).[178] No, no, no, that is not that! That is a misunderstanding in some way. In some respects, this is a misunderstanding that *dhyāna* [means that] you should do like this.[179]

PS DVD 4 (00:46:06)

ध्यानमनस्तमितं पुन-
रेष हि भगवान् विचित्ररूपाणि ।
सृजति तदेव ध्यानं
संकल्पालिखितसत्यरूपत्वम् ॥७७॥

dhyānam-anastamitaṁ punar-
eṣa hi bhagavān vicitra-rūpāṇi /
sṛjati tadeva dhyānaṁ
saṁkalpā-likhita-satya-rūpatvam //77//
[not recited in full]

Dhyānam-anastamitam, *dhyāna* is automatically going on. What is that *dhyāna*? *Eṣa hi bhagavān vicitra-rūpāṇim*, when you see doors, when you see windows, when you see gardeners, when you see everything, when you see toast, when you see [anything], it is *dhyāna*. It is *dhyāna* of Parabhairava, nothing else [laughs].

I am not to be blamed! You have to blame Abhinavagupta![180]

Viresh says, "I am sleepy. I want to sleep. I want to [play] basie-ball." What is that ball?

---

177 Meditation.
178 That is, *dhyāna* is not only an internal practice. [*Editor's note*]
179 Swamiji demonstrates the typical meditation in which one sits perfectly still, back erect, with eyes closed.
180 In a humerous and respectful way, Swamiji is saying that Abhinavagupta is to be blamed for this unique interpretation of what *dhyāna* really is. [*Editor's note*]

VIRESH: Baseball.

SWAMIJI: Baseball. And this is *dhyāna*. This is *samādhi*. This is *yoga*. This is everything. But you have to see it. And he sees it. Who?

DENISE: The person in the Parabhairava state.

SWAMIJI: One who is situated in that state of Parabhairava. What is *japa*[181] for him? *"Oṁ juṁ saḥ amṛteśvara bhairavāya namaḥ, oṁ juṁ saḥ . . ."*–this is not *japa*!

There is another system now. It has [been] created in the behavior of Abhinavagupta.

PS DVD 4 (00:47:33)

भुवनावलीं समस्तां
तत्त्वक्रमकल्पनामथाक्षगणम् ।
अन्तर्बोधे परिव-
र्तयति यत्सोऽस्य जप उदितः ॥७८॥

bhuvanāvalīṁ samastāṁ
tattva-krama-kalpanām-athākṣa-gaṇam /
antar-bodhe parivar-
tayati yatso'sya japa uditaḥ //78//

Bhuvanāvalīṁ samastāṁ, all *bhuvanās*, one hundred and eighteen worlds (for the time being, we will only conduct one hundred and eighteen worlds), these one hundred and eighteen worlds, and *tattva krama kalpanām*, and thirty-six elements, *athākṣagaṇam*, and along with all the organs which are existing in these one hundred and eighteen worlds, and *yat antar bodhe parivarta yati*, he behaves that all this is in *bodha*-Bhairava[182]; all exists in *bodha*-Bhairava, one by one, one by one, one by one.

There is *śāntātīta kalā* in Bhairava [along with] *śānta kalā*, *nivṛtti kalā*, *pratiṣṭhā kalā*, *Śiva tattva*, Sadāśiva, everything . . . and that mosquito.

181 Recitation of *mantra*.

182 "Bhairava filled with awareness." Swami Lakshmanjoo, Tantrāloka 1.122, USF archive. See also verse 16.

Antar bodhe parivarta yati, and he says, in his own *bodha*-Bhairava, he sees, one by one, he inserts everything in that. And that is *japa*, that is the [*mantra*], "*so'haṁ*". [Swamiji sings], "*So'haṁ, so'haṁ, so'haṁ śivo'haṁ. . . .*" Like that. This is that. It is not only [the mere recitation of] "*so'haṁ*". Everything is "*so'haṁ*".[183]

PS DVD 4 (00:49:30)

सर्वं समया दृष्ट्या
यत्पश्यति यच्च संविदं मनुते ।
विश्वश्मशाननिरतां
विग्रहखट्वाङ्गकल्पनाकलिताम् ॥७९॥
विश्वरसासवपूर्णं
निजकरगं वेद्यखण्डककपालम् ।
रसयति च यत्तदेतद्
व्रतमस्य सुदुर्लभं च सुलभं च ॥८०॥

sarvaṁ samayā dṛṣṭyā
yatpaśyati yacca saṁvidaṁ manute /
viśva-śmaśāna-niratāṁ
vigraha-khaṭvāṅga-kalpanākalitām //79//
viśva-rasāsava-pūrṇaṁ
nija-karagaṁ vedya-khaṇḍaka-kapālam /
rasayati ca yattadetad
vratam-asya sudurlabhaṁ ca sulabhaṁ ca //80//

These are two *ślokas* in one.

---

183 "It is *mantra* being recited from your mind, not with lips. "*So'haṁ*" is not to be recited with the lips, it is to be recited through breath." Swami Lakshmanjoo, *Tantrāloka* 15.133, USF archive.

"'*Oṁ so'haṁ*' is the *mantra* in which he resides in his remaining portion of his life. *Oṁ* is "I agree", *so'haṁ*, "I am one with that God consciousness". This is *murti mantra*, he becomes this kind of embodiment of that form, the form of God consciousness." Swami Lakshmanjoo, *Tantrāloka* 15.238, USF archive.

"His behavior", he says, "how . . . what is his behavior in this lifetime?"

Sarvaṁ samayā dṛṣṭyā, yat paśyati yacca saṁvidaṁ manute, viśva śmaśāna niratāṁ vigraha khaṭvāṅga kalpanākalitām. He sees that in this universe, the outside universe–outside the Parabhairava state, there is a universe–and it has become *smaśāna* (*smaśāna* means "graveyard"). This is a graveyard. This whole world is a graveyard. And his *vrata*[184] is just to dance in this graveyard.

JOHN: Cremation ground, is it?

SWAMIJI: Cremation ground, yes, for everybody! This is a graveyard because there are only skeletons going on [Swamiji imitates] everywhere, without the understanding of Parabhairava. When they don't understand Parabhairava, they are skeletons. And this is all *śmaśāna*, this is all a graveyard, where the cremation ground or that . . .

DENISE: Burial ground?

SWAMIJI: Where people are buried.

JONATHAN: Graveyard.

SWAMIJI: Graveyard. And for Europeans?

DEVOTEES: Graveyard.

SWAMIJI: Only graveyard?

DENISE: Cemetery.

SWAMIJI: And that, for Americans? "*Bzz, bzz, bzz, bzz*!" That is also a graveyard?

JONATHAN: Where they burn people.

GEORGE: Yes, that's a cremation.

DENISE: That is a crematorium.

SWAMIJI: That is also the same. This whole [universe] is filled with a graveyard. And, in the graveyard, he behaves and watches everything, and conducts everything, in each and every corner he goes on. This is his *vrata* in this *śmaśāna*.

Śmaśāna means, it is darkness. Although there is the light of the sun, there is the light of the moon, there is the light of the

---

184 Conduct.

stars, there is the light of candles, *bijley-wijley*[185], etc., but it is darkness because there is no understanding of Parabhairava's position in the real sense. So it is a *śmāśāna* (graveyard).

When Parabhairava walks, and takes a good walk, and a good examination, He examines the whole universe of His glory. This is his *vrata*, this is his conduct in the outside world. And it is *sudurlabhaṁ*, nobody can conduct this kind of [activity in the] outside world, but for him, it is very easy to conduct.

GEORGE: "Outside world" means when he comes out of his nature. When he's . . .

SWAMIJI: He never comes out of his nature. He comes out, but he has not come out. But he comes out in this nature also. At the same time, he is residing there also.

GEORGE: Is it *unmīlanā* and *nimīlanā*?

SWAMIJI: Yes, *unmīlanā-nimīlanā*[186] is a little bit [relevant here], but it is . . .

GEORGE: I just want to understand. When he comes out, this is the cremation ground?

SWAMIJI: This is like that. This is like that. Yes, it is like that, but in a broad way. "Broadway Hotel!"[187]

PS DVD 4 (00:54:20)

इति जन्मनाशहीनं
परमार्थमहेश्वराख्यमुपलभ्य ।

185 Electricity.

186 "*Unmīlanā samādhi* is experienced in *turyātīta* and *nimīlanā samādhi* is experienced in *turya*. This is the difference between *turya* and *turyātīta*. *Nimīlanā samādhi* means "absorption of universal consciousness"; when universal consciousness is absorbed in your nature, that is *turya*. When universal consciousness is expanded everywhere, that is *turyātīta* [viz., *unmīlanā samādhi*]." Swami Lakshmanjoo, *Tantrāloka* 10.288, USF archive. For an explanation of *turya* and *turyātīta*, see Appendix A-13.

187 Swamiji is joking. The Broadway Hotel is the name of a hotel in Srinagar, Kashmir.

उपलब्धृताप्रकाशात्
कृतकृत्यस्तिष्ठति यथेष्टम् ॥८१॥

iti janma-nāśa-hīnaṁ
paramārtha-maheśvarākhyam-upalabhya /
upalabdhṛtā-prakāśāt
kṛta-kṛtyas-tiṣṭhati yatheṣṭam //81//
[not recited or translated][188]

व्यापिनमभिहितमित्थं
सर्वात्मानं विधूतनानात्वम् ।
निरुपमपरमानन्दं
यो वेत्ति स तन्मयो भवति ॥८२॥

vyāpinam-abhihitam-itthaṁ
sarvātmānaṁ vidhūtanānātvam /
nirupama-paramānandaṁ
yo vetti sa tan-mayo bhavati //82//

In millions, there are thousands who are likely to be united with Parabhairava; *vyāpinam abhihitam itthaṁ sarvātmānaṁ vidhūtanānātvam*, who are all-pervading, who are not pervading only in one hundred and eighteen worlds, who are pervading outside that also; *vidhūtanānātvam*, who have shaken [off] altogether differentiatedness.

Viresh is different, you are different, you are different, you are different, you are different, you are different, everybody is different from each other. That differentiatedness is discarded, it is ended [for one] who has ended this differentiatedness. Who? He who resides in the Parabhairava state; in the Parabhairava state and without the Parabhairava state.

188 "Thus, realizing that which is called Maheśvara, the Absolute, which is free from birth and death, by the grace of the light of the nature of the perceiver, he remains, all his needs fulfilled, in accordance with his desires." *Paramārthasāra*, John Hughes (1972).

Nirupama param ānandaṁ, and joy (joy means that which has no *nirupama*, it has no comparison), *yo vetti*, if, God forbid, he tastes that, he comes to understand that *ānanda*, at the time of understanding, real understanding, he becomes one with that [bliss]. It catches him, it grabs him, and it is digested in him. That *ānanda*, Parabhairava is digested in *ānanda*.

There is only one. Parabhairava, he has digested Parabhairava in [one gulp][189], *bas*. This is the real way of Parabhairava.

Now [Abhinavagupta] goes down again in *māyā*.

PS DVD 4 (00:56:49)

तीर्थे श्वपचगृहे वा
नष्टस्मृतिरपि परित्यजन्देहम् ।

tīrthe śvapaca-gṛhe vā
naṣṭa-smṛtir-api parityajan-deham /*83a*

> Because he conducts both ways, up and down, up and down, up and down, up and down. This is up or only down. Or it is down, down, down, down. Or it is up, up, up. Or it is no, nothing [like] that. Everything![190]

Tīrthe, one who leaves his body near the Ganges, *śvapaca gṛhe vā*, he may [just as well] leave his body in a *wattal's* house . . .

You know?

DENISE: Sweeper's house.

SWAMIJI: A sweeper's house.

---

189 Swamiji makes the gesture of swallowing.

190 "*Sarvasarvātmakata*, take anything, it is full with everything. Take just a particle of just a germ, a small particle of a germ, a minute particle of a germ which cannot be experienced by your own eyes. That small germ, in the body of that small germ, you will find one hundred and eighteen worlds. This is the teaching of *Mālinī*." Swami Lakshmanjoo, *Paratriśika Vivaraṇa*, USF archive.

Here, Swamiji is refering to Parabhairava's behaviour, both above and below *māyā*. This state is referred to a *sarvasarvātmaka*, where all things are in one thing and one thing is in all things. [*Editor's note*]

. . . *naṣṭa smṛtir api*, if while leaving his body he cannot think of God.

ज्ञानसमकालमुक्तः
कैवल्यं याति हतशोकः ॥८३॥

jñāna-samakāla-muktaḥ
kaivalyaṁ yāti hata-śokaḥ //83//

At the time of his being united with God consciousness, there and then he is liberated from repeated births and deaths.[191] *Kaivalya yāti hataśokaḥ*, after leaving his body, he'll be sentenced to the state of Parabhairava. There is no . . .

[Abhinavagupta] has come down [i.e., regressed] again.

'हिमवति गङ्गाद्वारे
वाराणस्यां कुरौ प्रयागे वा ।
वेश्मनि चण्डालादेः
शिवतत्त्वविदां समं मरणम् ॥'

himavati gaṅgādvāre
vārāṇasyāṁ kurau prayāge vā /
veśmani caṇḍālādeḥ
śiva-tattva-vidāṁ samaṁ maraṇam //[192]

Himavati gaṅgādvāre, at the feet of the Ganges, *vārāṇasyāṁ*, in Kashi (Benares), *kurau*, in Kurukṣetra, *prayāge ca*, in Prayāg Allahabad, *veśmani caṇḍālādeḥ*, or in a butcher's house, *śiva*

191 "When a real Śaivite master, by the *śaktipāta* of Bhairava, penetrates anyone with grace . . . there and then, without *sādhana*, he becomes one with Him (Parabhairava). [This is that] initiation [in which you realize] that you are yourself no other than Bhairava." (Swami Lakshmanjoo's handwritten notes)
192 Quotation from *Śrī Nirvāṇayogottare* cited in Yogarāja's commentary.

tattva vidāṁ samaṁ maraṇam, [for] those who are situated in the Parabhairava state, there is no difference for them where to leave this body or where not to leave this body. They are sentenced in, pushed in, the Parabhairava state.

PS DVD 4 (00:59:45)

पुण्याय तीर्थसेवा
निरयाय श्वपचसदननिधनगतिः ।
पुण्यापुण्यकलङ्क
स्पर्शाभावे तु किं तेन ॥८४॥

puṇyāya tīrtha-sevā
nirayāya śvapaca-sadana-nidhana-gatiḥ /
puṇyāpuṇya-kalaṅka
sparśābhāve tu kiṁ tena //84//

Puṇyāya tīrthasevā, just being situated . . . some saints live only in *tīrtha* . . .

Tīrtha means . . . what is *tīrtha*?

JOHN: In temples, holy places.

SWAMIJI: Holy places, shrines.

. . . *tīrthe*, they live in shrines from childhood to the end of their lives just for the sake of liberation. That is for *puṇyāya*[193], for achieving the upper worlds, *svarga*, even the topmost *svargas* (heavens).

GEORGE: That *mahā loka, jana loka*, etc.[194]

SWAMIJI: Yes.

Śvapaca sadana nidhana gatiḥ nirayāya. And there is . . . if one lives in . . . [if] he goes and leaves his body in a butcher's house, *nirayāya gatiḥ*, he is sentenced to hell.

---

193 Merit.

194 The seven *lokas* (worlds) according to classical Hindu philosophy are *bhū*, *bhurvaḥ*, *svaḥ*, *mahaḥ*, *janaḥ*, *tapa*, and *satyaḥ*. According to Kashmir Shaivism, these seven *lokas* are limited and exist inside *nivṛtti kalā* or *pṛthvī aṇḍa*, where the element of earth predominates. [*Editor's note*] For an explanation of the five *kalās*, see Appendix A-8.

But the one who is above this, who has achieved the stage of Parabhairava, *puṇyāpuṇya kalaṅka sparśābhāve*, he has nothing of that to discriminate. "Where I shall leave the body?" It [makes no difference to him] to leave the body in Benaras or to leave the body in a butcher's house.

END Parmārthasara DVD 4 (01:02:08)

DVD 5

PS DVD 5 (00:00:01)

तुषकम्बुकसुपृथक्कृत-
    तण्डुलकणतुषदलान्तरक्षेपः ।
तण्डुलकणस्य कुरुते
    न पुनस्तद्रूपतादात्म्यम् ॥८५॥
तद्वत् कञ्चुकपटली-
    पृथक्कृता संविदत्र संस्कारात् ।
तिष्ठन्त्यपि मुक्तात्मा
    तत्स्पर्शविवर्जिता भवति ॥८६॥

tuṣa-kambuka-supṛthak-kṛta-
taṇḍula-kaṇa-tuṣa-dalāntara-kṣepaḥ /
taṇḍula-kaṇasya kurute
na punas-tad-rūpatād-ātmyam //85//
tadvat kañcukapaṭalī-
pṛthak-kṛtā saṁvidatra saṁskārāt /
tiṣṭhantyapi muktātmā
tat-sparśa-vivarjitā bhavati //86//

Tuṣa-kambuka-supṛthak-kṛta-taṇḍula-kaṇa-tuśa-dalāntara-kṣepaḥ. This *taṇḍula kaṇa* means the grain of rice which is already separated from all these three coverings. *Tuśa-dalāntara kṣepaḥ*, if you put that rice grain again in that . . .

DENISE: Husk.

SWAMIJI: . . . husk and everything, and wrap it with string and put it in the ground, it won't grow. In the same way, *tadvat kañcuka paṭalī pṛthak kṛtā saṁvidatra saṁskārāt*, in the same way, when the *kañcukas*, these *malas* (*āṇavamala*, *mayīyamala*, and *kārmamala*), when, by your *tīvra śaktipāta*[195], you are situated in God consciousness, . . .

And then what happens?

. . . *kañcuka paṭalī pṛthak kṛtā*, these coverings, three coverings, your consciousness is separated from these three coverings. *Saṁskārāt tiṣṭhantyapi*, although this body remains life-full for some period, *muktātmā*, you should not think that he is entangled by these *kañcukas*. *Tat sparśa vivarjitā*, he has nothing to do [with these]. This does not move him. This does not make him any different. If he is in *kañcuka* for some time, that does not [matter]. He is Parabhairava.

DENISE: Why would he ever be again in *kañcuka*?

SWAMIJI: Huh?

DENISE: Why would he be wrapped in *kañcuka*?

SWAMIJI: Just as I am! I am [in] *kañcuka*, e.g., I have got toothache, headache.

DENISE: But loosely.

SWAMIJI: Loosely. But I am not . . . I enjoy this.

PS DVD 5 (00:03:15)

कुशलतमशिल्पिकल्पित-
विमलीभावः समुद्गकोपाधेः ।
मलिनोऽपि मणिरुपाधे-
र्विच्छेदे स्वच्छपरमार्थः ॥८७॥

एवं सद्गुरुशासन-
विमलस्थिति वेदनं तनूपाधेः ।
मुक्तमप्युपाध्यन्तर-
शून्यमिवाभाति शिवरूपम् ॥८८॥

195 For an explanation of *śaktipāta* (grace), see Appendix A-7.

kuśalatama-śilpi-kalpita-
vimalī-bhāvaḥ samudgakopādheḥ /
malino'pi maṇir-upādher
vicchede svaccha-paramārthaḥ //87//
evaṁ sadguru-śāsana-
vimala-sthiti vedanaṁ tanūpādheḥ /
muktam-apy-upādhy-antara-
śūnyam-ivābhāti śiva-rūpam //88//

Kuśalatamaśilpi means the topmost *mani jñāni* (*mani jñāni* means *ratna jñāni*), who is the topmost jeweler.

If a jeweler has created that jewelry, the topmost, and he places that jewelry in *samudgaka* (*samudgaka* means one box, just a container), in a container, he puts that, *vicchede svaccha paramārtham*, as long as it is in the container, you don't see its glamour of shining, and it does not come out from that container, outside.

Evaṁ sadguru śāsana vimala . . .

It was an example. Now for the main point, what is the main point.

. . . *sadguru śāsana vimala sthiti vedanaṁ*, by the *śāsana*, by the treatment of a real *guru*, a real *sadguru*, master, your master, *vimala sthiti vedanaṁ*, when your knowledge, when your consciousness, is *vimala sthiti*, it has become shining, glittering, *tanūpādheḥ*, [even] if it is kept shining, but it is *tanūpādheḥ*, as long as the body is there–after the realization of this truth, as long as the body is there–it is stuck with the body [and] it does not show its effect outside. *Muktam api*, although this container, or this body, has no connection with that glamorous thing inside–it has no connection–but as long as the container is there, it does not reveal its shining contents outside.

And when this body is over, another container he does not get. When the body is over–at the time of death, the body is over–and, as other people [obtain] another container, a new container, so that shining thing is again wrapped in another life, and in the third life also, there is another container waiting for them, but this kind of system, he does not go under this. Who?

JOHN: This *jīvan mukta*, this Parabhairava.

DENISE: Parabhairava.

SWAMIJI: Parabhairava.

Because, as long as this one container is the last container–this is the last; you may call it the first and the last, the first container and the last container–there is no other container in which [he will enter], so it is shining, everywhere found.

PS DVD 5 (00:07:58)

शास्त्रादिप्रामाण्याद्
अविचलितश्रद्धयापि तन्मयताम् ।
प्राप्तः स एव पूर्वं
स्वर्गं नरकं मनुष्यत्वम् ॥८९॥

śāstrādi-prāmāṇyād
avicalita-śraddhayāpi tan-mayatām /
prāptaḥ sa eva pūrvaṁ
svargaṁ narakaṁ manuṣyatvam //89//

Śāstrādi prāmāṇyāt, by the [information] of the *śāstras* (scriptures) and by *śraddha* (faith), as [far] as that faith is concerned, the individual thinks [during his] lifetime, in the period of his lifetime also, that, "I'll be sentenced to *svarga* (heaven)" [or] "I'll be sentenced to *naraka*, I'll be sentenced to hell". He has got that faith because of his, that behavior, what he does. According to his behavior, he thinks in his mind that his future is not good or his future will be good. So, he understands before death that, "I'll go to heaven" [or] he understands before death that, "I will go to hell", and he goes to hell.

PS DVD 5 (00:09:30)

अन्त्यः क्षणस्तु तस्मिन्
पुण्यां पापां च वा स्थितिं पुष्यन् ।
मूढानां सहकारी
भावं गच्छति, गतौ तु न स हेतुः ॥९०॥

येऽपि तदात्मत्वेन विदुः
पशुपक्षिसरीसृपादयः स्वगतिम् ।
तेऽपि पुरातनसंबोध-
संस्कृतास्तां गतिं यान्ति ॥९१॥

antyaḥ kṣaṇas-tu tasmin
puṇyāṁ pāpāṁ ca vā sthitiṁ puṣyan /
mūḍhānāṁ sahakārī
bhāvaṁ gacchati, gatau tu na sa hetuḥ //90//

ye'pi tadātmatvena viduḥ
paśu-pakṣi-sarīsṛpādayaḥ svagatim /
te'pi purātana-saṁbodha-
saṁskṛtās-tāṁ gatiṁ yānti //91//

Antyaḥ kṣaṇastu, the last moment of death, *tasmin*, there, at that time, *puṇyāṁ pāpāṁ ca vā sthitiṁ puṣyan*, those who are ignorant persons, they collect–at that moment, the collection begins to gather–all their actions, good or bad. These collections are stored at the time of leaving his body, and this collection is stored there, and according to that collection, he is thrown . . . he goes to *svarga* (heaven) [or] he goes to *narak* (hell), or he goes to those rocks[196].

And there are some living beings–not only in human beings; in rocks also, in flies also, in birds also, in elephants also, *paśupakṣi sarīsṛpādayaḥ*, *sarīsṛpas* (snakes), everything–at the time of death, they, by the *śaktipāta–śaktipāta* (grace) behaves in them also–when He desires, when Parabhairava desires, that this brute bird should also get the state of Parabhairava, *te'pi purātana saṁbodha saṁskṛtās tāṁ gatiṁ yānti*, and they are pushed in the Parabhairava state in the end of their lives.

So, this *śaktipāta* is available in the market to everybody. But it is very difficult to have. It is dependent upon the *svātantrya śakti* of Parabhairava. If you do not desire [it], then it won't take

196 He is reborn as a rock.

place. If you desire [it], then it won't take [place]. This is the *svātantrya śakti* of Parabhairava.

JONATHAN: But at other times you have said it is indiscriminate. He can just give it to anyone, even whether they deserve or don't deserve. He can just [snap His fingers].

SWAMIJI: Yes, that is what I tell you again here also.

JONATHAN: But you just said, "If you desire it, then it's yours; if you don't desire it, that is also fine." I don't understand.[197]

SWAMIJI: That is also fine because it is your own wish. You don't like it. For the time being, you don't like to have Parabhairava. [You say], "What is the use of having the Parabhairava state? Why not eat, drink, and be merry, and be happy? I'll do this." This is also fine. This is one way of Parabhairava.

JOHN: But isn't it the grace of Parabhairava that you have the desire in the first place?

SWAMIJI: No, the second place also [laughing].

JOHN: And the first place also.

SWAMIJI: Yes, the first place also [laughing].

PS DVD 5 (00:13:29)

स्वर्गमयो निरयमय-
स्तदयं देहान्तरालगः पुरुषः ।
तद्भङ्गे स्वौचित्याद्
देहान्तरयोगमभ्येति ॥९२॥

एवं ज्ञानावसरे
स्वात्मा सकृदस्य यादृगवभातः ।
तादृश एव [तदासौ] सदासौ
न देहपातेऽन्यथा भवति ॥९३॥

197 Actually, Swamiji said that it won't be achieved in either case.

svargamayo niraya-mayas-
tadayaṁ dehāntarālagaḥ puruṣaḥ /
tadbhaṅge svaucityād
dehāntara-yogam-abhyeti / /*92*/ /
evaṁ jñānāvasare
svātmā sakṛd-asya yādṛg-avabhātaḥ /
tādṛśa eva sadāsau
na dehapāte'nyathā bhavati / /*93*/ /

It is "*tadāsau*" there. Abhinavagupta has written "*tadāsau*", but I have corrected it [to read] "*sadāsau*".

He has come down now again. He says, "What is the position when death takes place?"

[Here, Abhinavagupta has placed these two *ślokas*] for readers to know that, if *dhātu vaiṣamyāt*, . . .

Dhātu vaiṣamyāt means, at the time of death, *dhātu vaiṣam* takes place. That is when he is overwhelmed by acute pain of the death time because of *dhātu vaiṣamyāt*, when there is not equilibrium in the *nāḍīs* (veins), in the breath, and his memory is totally lost, and he cannot think anything about God, he cannot remember God at that time, because of too much pain. That occurs to some, this kind of pain, according to past actions.

. . . what happens at that time?

PS DVD 5 (00:15:44)

करणगणसंप्रमोषः
स्मृतिनाशः श्वासकलिलता च्छेदः ।
मर्मसु रुजाविशेषः
शरीरसंस्कारजो भोगः ॥९४॥
स कथं विग्रहयोगे
सति न भवेत्तेन मोहयोगेऽपि ।
मरणावसरे ज्ञानी
न च्यवते स्वात्मपरमार्थात् ॥९५॥

karaṇa-gaṇa-saṁpramoṣaḥ
smṛti-nāśaḥ śvāsa-kalilatā cchedaḥ /
marmasu rujā-viśeṣāḥ
śarīra-saṁskāra-jo bhogaḥ //94//
sa kathaṁ vigraha-yoge
sati na bhavet-tena moha-yoge'pi /
maraṇāvasare jñānī
na cyavate svātma-paramārthāt //95//
[not recited]

Karaṇa-gaṇa-saṁpramoṣaḥ, all the organs fail to function. I mean, the organs of action and the organs of cognition, they cannot act, they cannot perceive anything, whatever is going on at his death time, [on his] death bed. That is *karaṇa-gaṇa-saṁpramoṣaḥ*.

Just at one moment, he is aware and he sees his kith and kin watching him, but he cannot remember who is watching him. He is in a coma; he is absolutely sinking into a coma. And then he is again [aware for a moment but then he loses] his memory at once. If he thinks of somebody [for a moment, the very next moment] he forgets everything about him. *Smṛtināśaḥ*, memory does not survive. [If] memory survives, it appears and disappears at once.

Śvāsakalilatā (*śvāsakalilatā* means "hiccups"), he is overwhelmed by hiccups. [Excessive] hiccups are signs of leaving the body. Hiccups are not the result of good health. *Chedaḥ*, and sometimes there is the stoppage of the pulse (*chedaḥ*). *Marmasu rujā-viśeṣāḥ*, and in all his pores, he feels absolutely acute pain. He wants you to [massage] his body and, after pressing, he does not want you to press. He is neither satisfied with pressing nor satisfied with not-pressing. He cannot understand what has happened to [himself]. This is the *bhoga*, this is the last *bhoga* which is the death-*bhoga*[198]. It comes to somebody according to their past actions.[199]

198 Although *bhoga* can also mean "experience", Swamiji often translates *bhoga* as "enjoyment". [*Editor' note*]

199 "This is the reality of this body. There are *saṁbava-bhoga*, *janma-bhoga*, *sthiti-bhoga*–three ways of enjoyment in this body. First is *saṁbhava-bhoga*. *Saṁbhava-bhoga* means "existing in the womb".

Vigrahayoge, as far as the body is concerned, if he has a body, although he is situated in Parabhairava, *tena mohayoge'pi maraṇāvasare*, in this position also, *maraṇāvasare*, at the time of death, *jñānī*, the one who has observed, who has achieved, God consciousness, and who is situated in the Parabhairava state, *na cyavate jñāna svātma paramārthāt*, he is not deprived of that gain, that achievement. That achievement remains, that works. These things do not matter, [i.e., these ailments] of the death time.

GEORGE: "Matters" means? He still can have those signs but he is not affected by them.

SWAMIJI: He is not affected by them.

GEORGE: But he could go through all of those [ailments] just so it looks . . . to others.

SWAMIJI: Yes.

Janma-bhoga is when he comes out from the womb, he gets birth. Then *sthiti-bhoga*; *sthiti-bhoga* means "the span of his life". *Iti tisraḥ śarīrasya prāgavasthāḥ bhavanti*, these are three-fold states of the body in the beginning. . . . *Prasūtasya*, when he is born, then *bālyadivayaḥ pari-vṛttyā*, then traveling from childhood to youth, from youth to old age, from old age to lifelessness, [at which time] he always complains that he has no life in the joints, he has no life, he wants rest, he wants to take rest, don't disturb him. That is *sthiti-bhoga*, that is the enjoyment of [the span of one's] life. Then after life, there is another enjoyment that is called *mṛtyu-bhoga* (*mṛtyu-bhoga* means "the enjoyment of death"). When he dies, he enjoys that death, i.e., the pain, the pain he realizes, although it is killing pain, but still he enjoys that. . . . Then he *yiyāsutā*, [goes on a] journey for another world; *yiyāsutā* means "journey for other births". *Dve caramāvasthe*, and these are two states in the end–*mṛtyu-bhoga* and the journey, traveling. The point, what you think of that time, at that time of the journey, in the end, you go to that, you reach to that point. So it is worthwhile to remember Lord Śiva at that time when commencing that journey in the end." Swami Lakshmanjoo, *Janma Maraṇa Vicāra*, USF archive.

PS DVD 5 (00:19:59)

परमार्थमार्गमेनं
झटिति यदा गुरुमुखात् समभ्येति ।
अतितीव्रशक्तिपातात्
तदैव निर्विघ्नमेव शिवः ॥९६॥

paramārtha-mārgamenaṁ
jhaṭiti yadā guru-mukhāt samabhyeti /
atitīvra-śaktipātāt
tadaiva nirvighnam-eva śivaḥ //96//

Now, there is another way of behavior at the time of death. [Sometimes] something happens, something divine happens also to somebody at the time of death. [Even] if he has not done anything during the period of his lifetime, he has not [even] thought of doing some process of *yoga*, any process of *yoga*, and at the death time, the same position [i.e., establishment in the Parabhairava state] appears to him also. It is because he possesses a body. Although he has developed nothing in his lifetime, . . .

From his very birth, he has been about-turned to all these [spiritual] matters. He says, "It is all *bakwas*[200]! What is it? I don't believe in this. This '*paramārtha-swaramārtha*' is bogus".

. . . but, to him also, Parabhairava is such a great Being that to him also–it is not particularly always–sometimes to him also, to him also, at the time of death, [Parabhairava] thinks, "He should be relieved from the pangs of births and deaths. He should be one with Bhairava. I wish [this to be so]."

But there is no one to oppose [Him and say], "What has he done? If he has done nothing, why should You [liberate him]?"

"But, it is [My] will! It is My choice."

This also happens.

Paramārtha mārgamenaṁ jhaṭiti yadā guru mukhāt samabhyeti. *Guru* means, at that time, . . .

"Master" means Parabhairava's treatment. Here, *guru* does

200 Nonsense.

not mean [an actual *guru* because] he has undergone no *guru* right from his birth. He has not accepted any *guru* to guide him because he was against this guidance. He didn't want guidance of anything, and he didn't want to behave [in the] conduct of some spirituality because he had no faith in spirituality.

But, if Parabhairava thinks at the time of death also, "Let him become Parabhairava. It is My choice. I want to play with him like this", *atitīvra śaktipātāt*, and He infuses in him [with] *tīvra śaktipāta*, *tadaiva nirvighnameva śivaḥ*, *ekdum*[201] he flies and becomes one with Parabhairava.

So, all his ambitions are unwillingly fulfilled. He didn't wish for those kind of ambitions, and those are fulfilled. This is the treatment of Parabhairava, which is beyond *niyati* ("beyond *niyati*" means it is not due).

Yogarāja says, in his commentary, one example. He says, "The author"–*granthakāraṇa* means Abhinavagupta–"has also penned down this *śloka* for this":

हेलया क्रीडया वापि आदराद्वाथ तत्त्ववित् ।
यस्य संपातयेद् दृष्टिं स मुक्तस्तत्क्षणात्प्रिये ॥

helayā krīḍayā vāpi ādarādvātha tattvavit /
yasya saṁpātayed dṛṣṭiṁ sa muktas-tat-kṣaṇāt priye / /

Lord Śiva explains to Her, Bhairavī (Pārvatī), "O Pārvatī . . . "

It is penned down by Abhinavagupta, and this *śloka* is kept by Yogarāja, [the grand-disciple] of Abhinavagupta.

. . . Lord Śiva tells to Pārvatī, "O Pārvatī, it is not necessary that I have to be gracious to that person, that devotee of Mine, who has devotion for Me. That I do; for a devotional man, I behave like that [i.e., graciously]. But it is not always [on account of one's] devotion. *Helayā*, by play also, I play this kind of treatment (*krīḍayā*). *Ādarādvā*, with respect also, I play this treatment. *Yasya saṁpātayed dṛṣṭiṁ*, at once, when I see that he must become Parabhairava, he becomes Parabhairava, although his being Parabhairava is not due."

---

201 Hindi for "suddenly".

It [occurs] in [a person's] lifetime also, [not only at the time of death].

Now, another *śloka* is the ninety-seventh:

PS DVD 5 (00:26:53)

सर्वोत्तीर्णं रूपं
सोपानपदक्रमेण संश्रयतः ।
परतत्त्वरूढिलाभे
पर्यन्ते शिवमयीभावः ॥९७॥

sarvottīrṇaṁ rūpaṁ
sopāna-pada-krameṇa saṁśrayataḥ /
paratattva-rūḍhi-lābhe
paryante śivamayī-bhāvaḥ //97//

"Now, that devotee of Mine, *sarvottīrṇaṁ rūpaṁ*, . . . "

That *badhi bodha*[202] means "greater than the greatest", Parabhairava.

" . . . who does *abhyāsa*, who does *yoga* for the achievement of Parabhairava, *sopāna pada krameṇa*, successively, . . . "

Successively means steady and successively. As I told you, the scale of doing [*abhyāsa*] must be heavier than the ordinary activities of the world.

JONATHAN: You told us that.

SWAMIJI: Yes.

JOHN: Say that again, sir?

JONATHAN: On the scales, your practice of *abhyāsa* must be more than your practice of everyday, worldly activities. Swamiji told us.

SWAMIJI: ". . . *paratattva rūḍhi lābhe paryante śivamayī bhāvaḥ*, . . . "

This is the successive way.

" . . . and then, in the end, at the time of leaving his body, he is

---

202 "*Badhi bodha*" is a term that Swamiji used as a child to describe his experience of God consciousness.

united with Parabhairava. This is also the treatment which is due."

It is all according to the status of [His] government. That also stands.

JOHN: "Government" means?

SWAMIJI: The government of Parabhairava, the treatment of Parabhairava which [dispenses what] is due according [to a person's actions].

JOHN: This is *krama*?

SWAMIJI: This is *krama*, yes, the successive way. The unsuccessive way is also found there. Although it is not in that office like that, but it also is signed: "Oh, he must get it." If Kāla[203] says to Parabhairava, "He has not done any such deeds, Sir", [Parabhairava tells him], "Stop! It is done". He is Bhairava. So, He works like that.

And anyone who is Parabhairava in this field, he can also do this. It is not [only accomplished by] He, Parabhairava, that great Parabhairava, it is [also accomplished by] that small Parabhairava who has become Parabhairava. He'll also do the same treatment to everybody. There is not the slightest difference between that Parabhairava and this Parabhairava.

So, you should think like that also.

Now, it is [a further explanation of the successive way].

PS DVD 5 (00:30:09)

तस्य तु परमार्थमयीं
धारामगतस्य मध्यविश्रान्तेः ।
तत्पदलाभोत्सुक-
चेतसोऽपि मरणं कदाचित्स्यात् ॥९८॥

योगभ्रष्टः शास्त्रे
कथितोऽसौ चित्रभोगभुवनपतिः ।

203 Lit., time, Kāla, or Mahākāla, the Lord of time/death.

विश्रान्तिस्थानवशाद्
भूत्वा जन्मान्तरे शिवीभवति ॥९९॥

tasya tu paramārtha-mayīṁ
dhārām-agatasya madhya-viśrānteḥ /
tat-pada-lābhotsuka-
cetaso'pi maraṇaṁ kadācit-syāt / /98/ /
yoga-bhraṣṭaḥ śāstre
kathito'sau citra-bhoga-bhuvana-patiḥ /
viśrānti-sthāna-vaśād[204]
bhūtvā janmāntare śivī-bhavati / /99/ /

So, anybody who is successfully trying to find out the Parabhairava state through the *yogic* way of treatment, if, unfortunately, *dharām agatasya*, that supreme stage of Parabhairava he has not yet achieved in that life, in one lifetime, *madhya viśrānteḥ*, he who is stuck in the middle way, and who has no [desire] for worldly pleasures, for the enjoyment of worldly pleasures–he has absolutely discarded those worldly pleasures; he does not like those worldly pleasures–and he liked that *yoga* of Parabhairava, to achieve Parabhairava, [but] he has not the guts [for Its] achievement because his position of mind and the power of one-pointing his mind is very slow, and *madhya viśrānteḥ*, if he has half-way done this treatment [of *yoga*] and he [dies], he throws his body, . . .

Now, the thing is, what will happen to that person?

. . . *tat padalābha utsuka cetaso'pi*, already he has developed so much [desire] to achieve that state, *maraṇaṁ kadācitsyāt*, but, by his misfortune, he dies, what happens to him?

It is already explained in the *Bhagavad Gītā* also, through the question of Arjuna.[205]

Then, after death, *yoga bhraṣṭaḥ śāstre kathitaḥ*–in the *śāstras*, he is called *yoga bhraṣṭaḥ*; he is a *yoga bhraṣṭaḥ–asau*, this *yoga bhraṣṭaḥ*, after death, *citra bhoga bhuvana patiḥ*, he is pushed in the supreme highest paradises, highest . . .

---

204 Swamiji replaces "*vaśad*" with "*vaśād*". (Swami Lakshmanjoo's handwritten notes)

205 See *Bhagavad Gītā*, 6.41-43.

DENISE: Heavens.

SWAMIJI: . . . heavens, where Anantabhaṭṭāraka[206] is handling, and [this *yoga bhraṣṭaḥ*] is there, and *citra bhoga bhuvana patiḥ*, and he enjoys that . . .

Citra bhoga bhuvana patiḥ. There are two sections in the kingdom of Anantabhaṭṭāraka there. One section is the treatment of those who like only *abhyāsa* (practice), and another section is [for those] who like to enjoy the world also. He goes to that section, the second section.

. . . he enjoys in the way of worldly enjoyments there. And, after that, he is deputed by Anantabhaṭṭāraka in [the other] section where Anantabhaṭṭāraka asks [great] *yogīs* there [to] make him tread on the path of *nirvikalpa yoga* there.[207]

Bhūtvā janmāntare, then he comes, after a hundred and many million years, he comes here again, he is born [on earth], and, in that lifetime, he becomes Śiva, he becomes Parabhairava.

So, there is no fear for him. If he has not the capacity to do *yoga* and he has the desire to conduct *yoga*, he also will be glorified with My *śaktipāta*. So, there is no fear for anybody who, at any time, at any moment, takes My refuge.

PS DVD 5 (00:36:33)

परमार्थमार्गमेनं
ह्यभ्यस्याप्राप्य योगमपि नाम ।
सुरलोकभोगभागी
मुदितमना मोदते सुचिरम् ॥१००॥

विषयेषु सार्वभौमः
सर्वजनैः पूज्यते यथा राजा ।

206 "Anantabhaṭṭāraka is the personal assistant to Lord Śiva, the *rūdra* of Lord Śiva. He is Śiva but He is called Anantabhaṭṭāraka. Anantabhaṭṭāraka functions only in the inferior creation: in creation, protection, and destruction. Revealing and concealing, Lord Śiva handles Himself." Swami Lakshmanjoo, *Tantrāloka* 9.144, USF archive.

207 For an explanation of *nirvikalpa*, see Appendix A-11.

भुवनेषु सर्वदैवै-
 योगभ्रष्टस्तथा पूज्यः ॥१०१॥

paramārtha-mārgam-enaṁ
hy-abhyasyāprāpya yogam-api nāma /
sura-loka-bhoga-bhāgī
mudita-manā modate suciram //100//
viṣayeṣu sārva-bhaumaḥ
sarva-janaiḥ pūjyate yathā rājā /
bhuvaneṣu sarvadaivair
yoga-bhraṣṭas-tathā pūjyaḥ //101//

And there is a third section of *yoga bhraṣṭas* also, a third section [of one] who has got [much desire] to conduct worldly enjoyment fully, and who has got this desire also, acute desire, acute desire for *yoga* also. He who wants to conduct this and this both, for him, there is also a way, there is another third way for him. The third way is developed in that upper world. And that is another place of . . .

And that I was given in my last birth.

JOHN: In your last birth?

SWAMIJI: In my last birth, yes, I was given that.

JOHN: This time or the time before?

SWAMIJI: Before that.

DENISE: Before birth.

SWAMIJI: Before my birth, before this birth, when I was born when Abhinavagupta was born. I was also born with Abhinavagupta. I *was* Abhinavagupta, but I was not like that. I was just King Abhinavagupta in a past life. Now, I am not a king. I am Parabhairava.

JOHN: So, before Abhinavagupta was born, he came from this heaven, is it?

SWAMIJI: Yes.

JOHN: You came from this heaven?

SWAMIJI: Yes.

JOHN: And then Abhinavagupta lived his life, and then he left his body, . . .

SWAMIJI: Yes.

JOHN: . . . and then decided he had to come again?

SWAMIJI: Yes, then he entered in me. And then I was born again [as] Abhinavagupta, in this period.

JOHN: Now.

SWAMIJI: In that way, I was not Abhinavagupta. I was just simply a *yoga bhraṣṭa*. It does not mean Abhinavagupta is only one. Abhinavagupta can be many.

JOHN: How?

SWAMIJI: Because Parabhairava is also unlimited.

viṣayeṣu sārva-bhaumaḥ
sarva-janaiḥ pūjyate yathā rājā / *100a*
[repeated]

When I go [to] one world of paradise, all kings and queens make drum-beating and give me a salute–the kings and queens there. And I say, "Yes, good", and I go on, go on, in all those worlds, as if I have got a tour. I leave for a tour there and see the behavior of all the kings and queens, how they behave [towards] me, because I am crowned, I am the most valuable person. Like that.

PS DVD 5 (00:40:44)

bhuvaneṣu sarvadaivair
yoga-bhraṣṭas-tathā pūjyaḥ / / *101* / /
[repeated]

So, in all these heavens, those upper heavens, *yoga bhraṣṭaḥ tathā pūjyaḥ*, they all pay the greatest respect. But they don't give any of this . . . what is that?

GEORGE: Offerings.

SWAMIJI: Offering, they don't offer anything. But they, *bas*, respect. Because, at that time also, I didn't like to receive any offering. I like honor. And honor I developed there. I like that. It was my liking. This kind of *yoga bhraṣṭa* is also existing in this world. I have undergone many *yoga bhraṣṭas*.

JOHN: So this . . .
SWAMIJI: Yes, what?
DENISE: I wanted to listen to you.
SWAMIJI: [laughs]

PS DVD 5 (00:41:56)

महता कालेन पुन-
    र्मानुष्यं प्राप्य योगमभ्यस्य ।
प्राप्नोति दिव्यममृतं
    यस्मादावर्तते न पुनः ॥१०२॥

mahatā kālena punar-
    mānuṣyaṁ prāpya yogam-abhyasya /
prāpnoti divyam-amṛtaṁ
    yasmād-āvartate na punaḥ //102//

After many, many centuries, many, many million years, then he comes again in this world and achieves that divine nectar of Parabhairava, *yasmāt āvartate*, then he does not like to come again here.

And it will happen next, then I won't come [again in this world].

PS DVD 5 (00:42:39)

तस्मात् सन्मार्गेऽस्मिन्
    निरतो यः कश्चिदेति स शिवत्वम् ।
इति मत्वा परमार्थे
    यथातथापि प्रयतनीयम् ॥१०३॥

tasmāt sanmārge'smin
    nirato yaḥ kaścideti sa śivatvam /
iti matvā paramārthe
    yathā-tathāpi prayatanīyam //103//

"So, O my devotees," Abhinavagupta says to everybody, "O my devotees, *asmin sanmārge*, on this path of Parabhairava, the achievement of Parabhairava, whoever has taken a step with pure desire, no matter if that desire is slow or if that desire is intense or whatever it is, who has taken this step, who has tread on this step, . . ."

It does not matter if he is a *brahmin*, if he is a *wattal* (sweeper), if he is an outcast, if he is anybody, it does not matter for that.

". . . *nirato yaḥ kaścid eti sa śivatam*, he becomes one with Parabhairava. *Iti matvā*, this way you should take in your mind, *yathātathāpi prayatanīyam*, whatever happens, whatever may come, go on doing practice, go on doing practice. That practice may be the lowest practice, that practice may be medium practice, that practice may be intense practice, go on doing something, *yathātathāpi*, whatever comes."

If you are trodden down, go on doing, go on remembering God, go on remembering God. This is the way in which[ever] way you will remember [Him], *bas*, He will carry you, He will carry you. Because that remembrance is [the way]. It may be medium, it may be low, it may be very low, it may be the lowest, it may be intense, it may be very intense, that does not matter. Go on, another step, another step.

JOHN: Never stop trying.

SWAMIJI: *Yathātathāpi*, whatever happens.

JOHN: What's that number, sir? Number?

SWAMIJI: Number? Number 103.
Oh, "*evaṁ*". It is the ending.

एवं, शास्त्रकारः शेषभट्टारकोक्तं परमार्थसारोपदेशं
शिवाद्वयशासनक्रमेण युक्त्यनुभवागमसनाथं प्रतिपाद्य,
स्वात्मनः परितोषमात्रार्थितया स्वाभिधानप्रदर्शनपूर्वकम्
'अयमेव उपदेशः' इति निरूपयन् ग्रन्थार्थोपसंहारम् आह

evaṁ, this way, *śāstrakāraḥ śeṣabhaṭṭārakoktaṁ paramārthasāropadeśaṁ śivādvayaśāsanakrameṇa yuktyanubhavāgamasanāthaṁ pratipādya, svātmanaḥ paritoṣamātrārthitayā svābhidhānapradarśanapūrvakam 'ayameva upadeśaḥ' iti nirūpayan granthārthopasaṁhāram āha*[208]

Now, Abhinavagupta, the author of this book, says that it is the *nicoḍa*[209] of that Śeṣamuni's *Paramārthasāra*, . . .

Śeṣamuni's *Paramārthasāra*, you know? That Patañjali's *Paramārthasāra* which was the basis of this *Paramārthasāra*.

. . . and I have explained it with the whitewash of Shaivism. According to the Shaivite treatment, I have explained this *Paramārthasāra*. And the basis is that *Paramārthasāra* which was told to his disciple by Patañjali *muni*[210]."

PS DVD 5 (00:46:55)

इदमभिनवगुप्तोदित-
संक्षेपं ध्यायतः परं ब्रह्म ।
अचिरादेव शिवत्वं
निजहृदयावेशमभ्येति ॥१०४॥

idam-abhinavaguptodita-
saṁkṣepaṁ dhyāyataḥ paraṁ brahma /
acirād-eva śivatvaṁ
nija-hṛdayāveśam-abhyeti //104//
[not recited]

Idam abhinavagupta udita saṁkṣepam. This is the *saṁkṣepam*[211] only in one hundred *ślokas*. This *Paramārthasāra* I have kept in one hundred *ślokas*, in brief words. But, although it is one hundred *ślokas* in body, but in the volume of knowledge, it is

208 From Yogarāja's commentary.
209 Hindi for "extraction".
210 *Muni* means "saintly person".
211 *Saṁkṣepa* means an "extract" or "brief explanation".

more than one *crore ślokas*[212]. And that I have done in these few *ślokas*. This is my way of expanding and exposing in two words. I can expose the Parabhairava treatment, I can conduct the Parabhairava treatment, in two words! This is my power (Abhinavagupta says). And which two words, Lord Śiva and Pārvatī could not explain it in one *crore ślokas*. They have explained that knowledge in one *crore ślokas*, one hundred thousand *ślokas*–more than that. Mine is the power which gives [that knowledge] in two words, and one becomes, at once, before it is inserted in his brain, before that, he becomes Bhairava.

This is the treatment of that "electronic treatment". Once Abhinavagupta is here and Abhinavagupta has uttered no word yet, he is going to utter, and if he is going to utter, *bas*, there and then [the disciple] becomes Bhairava! So, at that time, nobody hears afterwards. His disciple won't hear anything. And Abhinavagupta will hear what he [himself] is speaking. [The disciple] is gone, he is gone before that. Where?

DENISE: Into the state of Parabhairava.

SWAMIJI: Yes. This is Abhinavagupta's power of treatment. So, where there is Abhinavagupta, there is everything. Parabhairava is also struck with amazement in seeing Abhinavagupta. Abhinavagupta is that being who came and got [that] treatment in the upper world also, and he has come [to this world] for that treatment.

JOHN: What are those two words?

SWAMIJI: Huh? [laughter]

GEORGE: Parabhairava.

SWAMIJI: Parabhairava, no. It is his . . . he just . . . if he . . .

JOHN: Yes, in other words, he is not telling us because we are all . . .

SWAMIJI: No. Like that, if you [record me on the video camera] and I don't speak anything–you only conduct the machinery–without speaking, it comes in that. Without my speaking, it comes in that. Do you understand? Everything comes in that. And, when I speak, it does not come in that. It goes in the ether. You can take it in the hand to the United States with this

212 One crore is equal to ten million.

videotape. The videotape will be there.

JOHN: So these are unspoken words.

SWAMIJI: Unspoken words.

JOHN: Two unspoken words.

SWAMIJI: "Two"–not [laughter]! "Two" does not mean "two".

DENISE: It means his power is so great that even if he said two words, you would go into that state before he said the words.

SWAMIJI: Yes.

PS DVD 5 (00:51:18)

आर्याशतेन तदिदं
संक्षिप्तं शास्त्रसारमतिगूढम् ।
अभिनवगुप्तेन मया
शिवचरणस्मरणदीप्तेन ॥१०५॥

āryā-śatena tadidaṁ
saṁkṣiptaṁ śāstra-sāram-atigūḍham /
abhinavaguptena mayā
śiva-caraṇa-smaraṇa-dīptena //105//

Mayā abhinavaguptena, I, Abhinavagupta, who am *dīptena* (shining, glittering) by being united with the millions of energies of Parabhairava (*śiva caraṇa smaraṇa dīptena*, he is brilliantly shining), and I, Abhinavagupta, have *saṁkṣiptaṁ*, spoken in brief words the essence of all *śāstras*! Whatever exists, whatever does not exist, whatever is to be published, whatever is coming, another treatment of *śāstra* which will come in the future, that too is shining here in this, in the *Paramārthasāra*, in these one hundred *ślokas*.

Now, there is the *śloka* of the commentator, Yogarāja:

श्रीमतः क्षेमराजस्य सद्गुर्वाम्नायशालिनः ।
साक्षात्कृतमहेशस्य तस्यान्तेवासिना मया ॥१॥

श्रीवितस्तापुरीधाम्ना विरक्तेन तपस्विना ।
विवृतिर्योगनाम्नेयं पूर्णाद्वयमयी कृता ॥२॥

śrīmataḥ kṣemarājasya sadgurvāmnāya-śālinaḥ /
sākṣātkṛta-maheśasya tasyāntevāsinā mayā //1//

śrī-vitastā-purī-dhāmnā viraktena tapasvinā /
vivṛtir-yoganāmneyaṁ pūrṇādvayamayī kṛtā //2//

Yogarāja says, "My master, who was Kṣemarāja, who was *sadgurvāmnāyaśālinaḥ*, who was my master, *sākṣātkṛta maheśasya tasyāntevāsinā mayā*, and he was the *śiṣya* (disciple), my master was the *śiṣya* of that person who had become one with Parabhairava." That is, Abhinavagupta. "He was his *śiṣya*; my master was his *śiṣya*. And I was *virakta*, I was a *brahmacārī*."

Who? Yogarāja.

Yogarāja [says], "I was a *brahmacārī*, and I was living near Lalitapura on the shore of the river Jelum near Bijbehara."

Bijbehara is where there are those *jyotiṣis* (astrologers).

"*Vivṛtir yoganāmneyaṁ pūrṇādvayamayī kṛtā. Yoganāmna*, and my name [is] Yogarāja, and I have done this *vivṛti tīkha* (brief commentary) of my grand-master's work.

Who is [his] grand-master?

GEORGE: Abhinavagupta.

SWAMIJI: Abhinavagupta.

[सं]परि पूर्णेयं परमार्थसारसंक्षिप्ता[ग्रह]विवृतिः
कृतिस्तत्रभवत्परममाहेश्वर श्रीराजाकयोगराजस्य ॥

[saṁ] pari pūrṇeyaṁ paramārthasāra saṁkṣiptā [graha] vivṛtiḥ kṛtistatra bhavat parama māheśvara śrī rājānaka yogarājasya //

This is the work of Yogarāja, i.e., this commentary.

इति शिवं

iti śivaṁ[213]

Bas, it is done.

END Paramārthasara DVD 5 (00:55:24)

Jai Guru Dev!

———o———

213 "*Iti śivaṁ*, Lord Śiva will remain always." Swami Lakshmanjoo, *Bhagavad Gītā* audio, USF archive.

Appendix A

1. *Prakṛti and the guṇas*

That individual you can't find in this world–or, right from heaven to this mortal world–you won't find such an individual existing who has not come in the grip of the three *guṇas*. So, everybody, whoever is existing in this world or in the heavens, are entangled in the cycle of three *guṇas*, the three *guṇas* [which are] born from *prakṛti*."

Swami Lakshmanjoo, *Bhagavad Gītā* audio, USF archive.

[*Prakṛti* is] the undifferentiated (*avyakta*, unmanifested) state of the three *guṇas*; *prakṛti* is the womb of three *guṇas*.

In *prakṛti*, you can't see the three *guṇas*. So you have to agitate that . . . [And agitation is done by] Anantabhaṭṭāraka or Śrīkaṇṭhanātha . . . and that is the state of *guṇa tattva* not *prakṛti tattva*. *Prakṛti tattva* is the un-agitated state and *guṇa tattva* is the agitated state. It is why in Shaivism, we have put another element of *guṇa tattva*. So *prakṛti* creates that *guṇa tattva*. But in *prakṛti*, *guṇa tattva* is not visible [because] it is mixed. *Prakṛti* is the mixture of three *guṇas*. [*Prakṛti* is] wherefrom the *guṇas* will come out. *Prakṛti* is the womb of the three *guṇas*.

Prakṛti is called "*sāmyavastha*", the equilibrium state of *sukha*, *duḥkha*, and *moha* [viz., *sāttvaguṇa*, *rājoguṇa*, and *tāmoguṇa*]. And *prakṛti* is *karaṇa*, *prakṛti* is the cause, and the effect is *sukha*, *duḥkha*, and *moha*–pleasure, pain, and illusion (the unconscious state).

Prakṛti is an objective element. *Prakṛti* is to be enjoyed by the enjoyer. The enjoyer is *puruṣa* entangled with five subjective elements [i.e., the *kañcukas*].

Prakṛti is our nature. And that nature is limited by our intellect, which is the collection of *sāttvaguṇa*, *rājoguṇa*, and *tāmoguṇa*. *Prakṛti* is always wavering in the *guṇas*. Sometimes you are sad, sometimes you are joyous, sometimes you are giddy.

That is *prakṛti*.

Prakṛti is always different, for every person, each and every person.

Swami Lakshmanjoo, *Tantrāloka* 9.215-223, USF archive.

These three tides of the three *guṇas* are, in the real sense, one with God consciousness."

Swami Lakshmanjoo, *Bhagavad Gītā* audio, USF archive.

Prakṛti is explained in the *śāstras* (scriptures) in two ways. *Aparā prakṛti*, which is said to be eightfold, is the combination of the five great elements, along with the mind, intellect, and ego. *Parā prakṛti* is that energy of being which governs and contains all the activities and conceptions of this universe.

Kashmir Shaivism–The Secret Supreme, 14.95.

. . . the five elements, mind, intellect, and ego. This is *aṣṭadhā*, the eightfold *prakṛti. Prakṛti* means My *śakti*, but *apareyam*, this is *aparā* (gross).

And there is another one which is a subtle *śakti*. That is *parā prakṛti*, supreme *prakṛti*, supreme energy that is *svātantya śakti*; by which *svātantrya śakti* this whole universe is standing, is fixed. *Parā prakṛti* takes hold of the whole universe, whatever is and whatever is not existing.

Aparā prakṛti is just for the inferior scale. That is eightfold. The five elements, mind, intellect, and ego, this is called *aparā prakṛti*. And *parā prakṛti* is supreme, that is *svātantya śakti* by which this whole universe and I am also existing. That [*parā*] *śakti* is My personal property. And this *aparā śakti* is the property of Anantabhāṭṭaraka. He has to deal with that *śakti* according to the good *karmas* and the bad *karmas* of individual beings. And by that, he creates them, he protects them, and he destroys them. And this great *prakṛti*, which is *svātantrya śakti*, by that, I conceal and reveal My nature to them.

Pidanā (concealing) and *anugraha* (revealing), I deal with that *svātantrya śakti*. The rest (creation, protection and destruction) is done according to your own *karmas*, and the operator is Anantabhāṭṭaraka.

[So], this *aparā prakṛti* is held and understood by everybody–this inferior *prakṛti*. This *prakṛti* has created this universe and

[has] protected and destroyed [it] from time to time. And the life of this *prakṛti* is separate, dwelling in My *parā prakṛti*. This is how the creation and these five-fold acts of this universe take place; the three-fold acts by inferior *prakṛti* and the other two fold acts by supreme [*prakṛti*].

Bhagavad Gītā 7.5, with commentary.

Prakṛti and *puruṣa* both are beginning-less and endless. *Prakṛti* is endless and beginning-less and *puruṣa* is endless and beginning-less. Both are endless and beginning-less, but *vikārāṁśca guṇāṁścaiva viddhi prakṛti saṁbhavān*, the three *guṇas* and the *ghaṭa padādi*, all of the objective world is produced by *prakṛti*. *Prakṛti* has produced these flowers; these houses, plants, motorcars, all other things, they are produced by *prakṛti*. And *prakṛti* has nothing to do with this production.

Prakṛti has made this for *puruṣa* to taste so that he will be entangled in the wheel of repeated births and deaths. *Prakṛti* is dumb, quiet–she is *jaḍa* (inert). She creates this for *puruṣa*. As soon as *puruṣa* gets awareness of *prakṛti* that, "*Prakṛti* is dancing on me", he becomes *mukta* and he remains aloof from *prakṛti*. Then he enters into the state of Parabhairava and he is *jīvan mukta* (liberated while embodied).

As long as *prakṛti* is not aware that he knows me, . . .

Who? *Puruṣa*.

. . . she dances, she kicks him, she plays him, from one birth to another birth, from another birth to another birth, whatever she likes. But, as soon as he is aware of *prakṛti*, [that] "*Prakṛti* is playing with me", he becomes *jīvan mukta* at once.

Bhagavad Gītā 13.20-21, with commentary.

2. *Svātantrya*

All these five energies of God consciousness are produced by His *svātantrya śakti* of freedom, His free power. That is called *svātantrya śakti*. *Svātantrya śakti* produces these five energies of Lord Śiva. And *cit śakti* is actually based on His nature, *ānanda śakti* is based on His *śakti*, on His Pārvatī, *icchā śakti* is based in *Sādaśiva*, and *jñāna śakti* (the energy of knowledge) is based on *Īśvara*, and the energy of *kriyā* is based on *Śuddhāvidya*. All these five pure states of Lord Śiva are one with Lord Śiva. *Cit śakti* indicates Lord Siva's actual position, *ānanda śakti* indicates Lord Śiva's position of *śakti*, and *icchā śakti* indicates Lord Śiva's position of *Sādaśiva*, and *jñāna śakti* indicates His position of *Īśvara*, and *Śuddhāvidya* is [His] fifth position [viz., *kriyā śakti*]. All these five positions are filled with God consciousness. Below that is the scale of *māyā*, illusion. That will go from *māya* to earth.

Swami Lakshmanjoo, *Special Verses on Practice*, USF archive.

The definition of *svātantrya* is "freedom in action and freedom in knowledge"; when you know with your freedom, when you act with your freedom. When you know and you don't succeed in that knowledge, there is not *svātantrya*. When there is not *svātantrya*, it is not really knowledge. When there is not *svātantrya*, it is not really action. The action of individuals is just like that. Individuals know, they know something–you can't say that they don't know anything–they know something, but that knowledge has not *svātantrya*. And they act also, they do something, but that doing also has not *svātantrya*. So, without *svātantrya*, doing and knowing has no value. When there is *svātantrya*, it is fully valued.

That essence of *svātantrya* is *anavacchinna* (beyond limitation), all-round beyond limitation. There is no such limit found in that state. *Vicchinna camatkāra maya viśrāntyā*, and this limited state of being is also found there. [Lord Śiva] is unlimited, but the limited cycle of God consciousness is also found there. So it is both limited and unlimited. That being who is limited only, he is not true. That being who is unlimited only, he is not true. Why? Because he is limited. The being who is unlimited is not true because he is unlimited only [and] not limited. That fullness of God consciousness is found [in one] who is limited and, at the same time, unlimited also. That is the fullness of God consciousness. The fullness of God consciousness is where nothing is excluded. Whatever is excluded, it is also one with that. That is the fullness of God consciousness.

Swami Lakshmanjoo, *Parātrīśikā Vivaraṇa* audio with commentary, USF archive.

Lord Śiva creates this external universe for the sake of realizing His own nature. That is why this external universe is called

"Sakti", because it is the means to realize one's own nature. Therefore, in order to recognize His nature, He must first become ignorant of His nature. Only then can He recognize it.

Why should He want to recognize His nature in the first place? It is because of His freedom, His *svātantrya* (independence). This is the play of the universe. This universe was created solely for the fun and joy of this realization. It happens that when His fullness overflows, He wants to [become] incomplete. He wants to appear as being incomplete just so He can achieve completion. This is the play of His *svātantrya*: to depart from His own nature in order to enjoy it again. It is this *svātantrya* that has created this whole universe. This is the play of Śiva's *svātantrya*.

This kind of action cannot be accomplished by any power in this universe other than Lord Śiva. Only Lord Śiva can do this. Only Lord Śiva, by His own *svātantrya*, can totally ignore and mask His own nature. This is His *svātantrya*, His glory, His intelligence. Intelligence does not mean that in this super-drama called creation you will only play the part of a lady or a man. With this kind of intelligence, you will also play the part of rocks, of trees, of all things. This kind of intelligence is found only in the state of Lord Śiva and nowhere else.

Self Realization in Kashmir Shaivism–Fifteen Verses of Wisdom, chapter 1, Verses 5, 6 and 7, pp23-26.

Svātantrya śakti and *māyā* are one. *Svātantrya śakti* is that state of energy which can produce the power of going down and coming up again. And *māyā* is not like that. *Māyā* will give you the strength of coming down and then no ability of going up. Then you cannot go up again. This is the state of *māyā*. And all these three *malas* ("impurities") reside in *māyā śākti*, not *svātantrya śakti*, although *svātantrya śakti* and *māyā śakti* are one. *Māyā śakti* is that energy, universal energy, which is owned by the individual being, the individual soul. The same energy, when it is owned by the universal Being, is called *svātantrya śakti*.

Svātantrya śakti is pure universal energy. Impure universal energy is *māyā*. It is only the formation that changes through a difference of vision. When you experience *svātantrya śakti* in a crooked way, it becomes *māyā śakti* for you. And when you realize that same *māyā śakti* in Reality, then that *māyā śakti* becomes *svātantrya śakti* for you. Therefore, *svātantrya śakti* and *māyā śakti* are actually only one and the three impurities (*malas*), which are to be explained here, reside in *māyā śakti*, not in *svātantrya śakti*.

Kashmir Shaivism–The Secret Supreme, 7.47.

3. ***Malas***

The three impurities are gross (*sthūla*), subtle (*sūkṣma*), and subtlest (*para*). The gross impurity is called *kārmamala*. It is connected with actions. It is that impurity which inserts impressions such as those which are expressed in the statements, "I am happy", "I am not well", "I have pain", "I am a great man", "I am really lucky", etc., in the consciousness of the individual being.

The next impurity is called *māyīyamala*. This impurity creates differentiation in one's own consciousness. It is the impurity of ignorance (*avidyā*), the subtle impurity. The thoughts, "This house is mine", "That house is not mine", "This man is my friend", "That man is my enemy", "She is my wife", "She is not my wife", are all created by *māyīyamala*. *Māyīyamala* creates duality.

The third impurity is called *āṇavamala*. It is the subtlest impurity.* *Āṇavamala* is the particular internal impurity of the individual. Although he reaches the nearest state of the consciousness of Śiva, he has no ability to catch hold of that state. That inability is the creation of *āṇavamala*. For example, if you are conscious of your own nature and then that consciousness fades away, and fades away quickly, this fading is caused by *āṇavamala*.

Āṇavamala is *apūrṇatā*, non-fullness. It is the feeling of being incomplete. Due to this impurity, you feel incomplete in every way. . . . Though you feel incomplete, knowing that there is some lack in you, yet you do not know what this lack really is. You want to hold everything, and yet no matter what you hold, you do not fill your sense of lacking, your gap. You cannot fill this lacking unless the master points it out to you and then carries you to that point.

Of these three impurities, *āṇavamala* and *māyīyamala* are not in action, they are only in perception, in experience. It is *kārmamala* which is in action.

Kashmir Shaivism–The Secret Supreme, 7.47-49.

*Aṇavamala is the root of the other two impurities. Which are those other two impurities? *Māyīyamala* and *kārmamala*.
Swami Lakshmanjoo, *Parātrīśikā Vivaraṇa*, USF archive.

This whole universal existence, which is admitted by other thinkers, that it is ignorance, that it is *māyā* (illusion), that is pain, it is torture–they explain it like that–but we Shaivites don't explain like that. We Shaivites explain that this [universe] is the expansion of your own nature. *Mala* is nothing; *mala* is only your free will of expanding your own nature.

So we have come to this conclusion that *mala* is not a real impurity [i.e., substance]. It is your own choice; it is the choice of Lord Śiva. The existence of impurity is just the choice of Lord Śiva, it is not some thing. It is *svarūpa svātantrya māṭraṁ*, it is just your will, just your independent glory.

If you realize that it is *svarūpa svātantrya māṭraṁ*, [that] it is your own play, then what will an impure thing do? An impure thing will only infuse purity in you . . . if you realize that impurity is not existing at all, it is just your own play, just your own independent expansion.

[So], *mala* is neither formless nor with form. It is just ignorance. It doesn't allow knowledge to function; knowledge is stopped. *Mala* is the absence of knowledge. *Mala* is not something substantial. . . . So, this absence of knowledge takes place only by ignorance . . . otherwise there is no *mala*. In the real sense, *mala* does not exist, impurity does not exist.
Swami Lakshmanjoo, *Tantrāloka* 9.79-83, USF archives.

4. ***Kañcukas*** **(lit., coverings).**

Directly, universal consciousness can never travel to individual consciousness unless universal consciousness is absolutely disconnected. *Māyā* is the disconnecting element from God consciousness. *Kalā* (limited action) is the connecting element to that dead being in some limited thing. So he does something by *kalā*. When he does something, then individuality shines. Otherwise, direct from God consciousness, individual consciousness would never come in existence.
Swami Lakshmanjoo, *Tantrāloka* 9.175-6, USF archive.

Kalā, *vidyā*, *rāga*, *kāla*, and *niyati* are the limiting connecting rods [between the individual and God].
Swami Lakhmanjoo, Tantrāloka 9.257, USF archive. For a further explanation of the *ṣaṭ kañcukas* (the six coverings), see *Kashmir Shaivism–The Secret Supreme*, 1.7-8.

[The five pure states of Lord Śiva] take the formation of *ṣaṭ kañcuka* in the individual. Because, whatever is manifested in the universe, it is not manifested [as] other than Śiva. The same thing has come out in manifestation; the same thing what existed in Paramaśiva, that same thing is manifested outside also."
Swami Lakshmanjoo, *Tantrāloka* 6.41, USF archive.

Kalā, *vidyā*, *rāga*, *kāla*, and *niyati*, these five elements are just offsprings of, offshoots of, *māyā*. *Kalā* means, "the capacity of doing something", *vidyā* means "the capacity of knowing something", *rāga* means "the capacity of some attachment (not universal attachment)", *niyati* means "the capacity of the limitation of space", *Kāla* means "the limitation of time".
Swami Lakshmanjoo, *Tantrāloka* 9.41, USF archive.

These [*kañcukas*] are pertaining to the individual being. It is why [the grammarian] Pāṇini has also accepted these, the representatives of these [*kañcukas* as the letters] *ya*, *ra*, *la*, *va*; these letters as *antaḥstha*. . . . And all these [subtle] energies are found, not outside the individual being, but inside the individual being, inside the thought of the individual being, inside the perception of the individual being. So they are named, nominated, by the grammarian [Pāṇini], as "*antaḥstha*". *Antaḥstha* means "that which is residing inside of the individual being". . . . We say that it is not *antaḥstha*, it is *dhāraṇā* [lit., the bearing or support] because it gives *life* to individual being. The individual being is created, the individual being is glorified, by these five elements ("five" means the five coverings); the glory of his own place, not the glory of Śiva; glorified with his own . . . that limited sphere.
Swami Lakshmanjoo, *Shiva Sutra Vimarśinī*, USF archive.

In [Śaiva] *tantras*, they are nominated as "*dhāraṇā*". These five elements (*kalā*, *vidyā*, *rāga*, *kāla*, *niyati*, with *māyā*) are called "*dhāraṇā*" because they give life to the individual being; the individual being lives in these five elements. Without these five elements, there was no life to individual being, there was only the sphere of Lord Śiva. If these five elements would not be there, there was no question of the individual being to exist. The individual being lives only on the basis of these five elements. So they are nominated as *dhāraṇā*. *Dhāraṇā* means, that which gives you life to exist.

Swami Lakshmanjoo, *Śiva Sūtra Vimarśinī*, USF archive. See also *Kashmir Shaivism–The Secret Supreme*, 1.7.

5. **The Seven Perceivers**

The first state is called *sakala*. The *sakala* state is that state where perception takes place in the objective world and not in the subjective world. In other words, I would call this state the state of *prameya,* the state of the object of perception. It is realized by its *pramātṛ*, the observer who resides in this state, in the field of objectivity and its world.

The second state is called *pralayākala*. This is the state of negation, where the whole world is negated. And the one who resides in this world of negation is called *pralayākala pramātṛ*, the observer of the *pralayākala* state. And this *pramātṛ*, this perceiver, does not experience the state of this voidness because it is actually the state of unawareness. This state would be observed at the time of *mūrcchā*, when one becomes comatose, which is like unnatural and heavy sleep, like deep sleep devoid of dreams. And the observer, *pralayākala pramātṛ*, resides in that void of unawareness. These two states [*sakala* and *pralayākala*] function in the state of individuality, not in the state of your real nature. These are states of worldly people, not spiritual aspirants.

The third state is called *vijñānākala pramātṛ*. This state is experienced by those who are on the path of *yoga*. Here, the *yogī* experiences awareness at times (but this awareness is not active awareness), and at other times, his awareness is active but he is not aware of that active awareness. This *vijñānākala pramātṛ*, therefore, takes place in two ways: sometimes it is full of action (*svātantrya*) without awareness, and sometimes it is full of awareness without action.

The fourth state of the observer is called *śuddhavidyā* and its observer is called *mantra pramātṛ*. In this state, the observer is always aware with *svātantrya*.

The next state is called *īśvara* and its observer is called *mantreśvara pramātṛ*. The word "*mantreśvara*" means "the one who has sovereignty on *mantra* (*ahaṁ*–I)." This state is like that of *mantra pramātṛ*, full of consciousness, full of bliss, full of will, full of knowledge, and full of action, however, this is a more stable state. The aspirant finds more stability here. The *mantra* for this state is "*idaṁ-ahaṁ*". The meaning of this *mantra* is that the aspirant feels that this whole universe is not false. On the contrary, he feels that this whole universe is the expansion of his own nature. In the state of *mantra pramātṛ*, he felt that the universe was false, that he was the truth of this reality. Now he unites the state of the universe with the state of his own consciousness. This is actually the unification of *jīva*, the individual, with Śiva, the universal.

The next state is the state of *sadāśiva*. The observer of this state is called *mantra maheśvara*. In this state, the observer finds himself to be absolutely one with the universal transcendental Being. He experiences this state to be more valid, more solid, and deserving of confidence. Once he enters into this state, there is no question at all of falling from it. This is the established state of his Self, his own Real nature. The *mantra* of this state is "*ahaṁ-idaṁ*". The meaning of this *mantra* is, "I am this universe." Here, he finds his Self in the universe, while in the previous state of *mantreśvara*, he found the universe in his Self. This is the difference.

The seventh and last state is the state of Śiva and the observer of this state is no other than Śiva Himself. In the other six, the state is one thing and the observer is something else. In this final state, the state is Śiva and the observer is also Śiva. There is nothing outside Śiva. The *mantra* in this state is "*ahaṁ*", universal-I. This-ness is gone, melted in His I-ness. This state is completely filled with consciousness, bliss, will, knowledge, and action.

Kashmir Shaivism–The Secret Supreme, 8.51-54.

6. *Upāyas* (the "means" or "ways")

The difference between *āṇavopāya*, *śāktopāya*, and *śāmbhavopāya* is this: In *āṇavopāya*, the strength of your awareness is such that you have to take the support of everything as an aid to maintain and strengthen your awareness. In *śāktopāya*, your awareness is strengthened to the extent that only one point is needed as a support for your concentration and that point is the center. In *śāmbhavopya*, the strength of your awareness is such that no support is needed. You are already residing in the meant (*upeya*). There is nowhere to go, just reside at your own point. The rest is automatic.

It is important to realize that though there are different *upāyas*, all lead you to the state of one transcendental consciousness. The difference in these *upāyas* is that *āṇavopāya* will carry you in a long way, *śāktopāya* in a shorter way, and *śāmbhavopāya* in the shortest way. Although the ways are different, the point to be achieved is one.

Kashmir Shaivism–The Secret Supreme, 5.39-40.

7. *Śaktipāta*

The five great acts of Lord Śiva are *sṛṣṭi* (the creative act), *sthiti* (the protective act), *saṁhāra* (the destructive act), *tirodhāna* (the act of enfolding or concealing His nature), and *anugraha* (the act of unfolding or revealing His nature).

In the kingdom of spirituality, Lord Śiva creates masters and disciples through His fifth act, the act of grace (*anugraha*). This grace is ninefold and, therefore, He creates masters and disciples in nine different ways.

The first and highest level of grace is called "*tīvratīvra śaktipāta*". *Tīvratīvra śaktipāta* means "super-supreme grace". When Lord Śiva bestows super-supreme grace on anyone, then that person becomes perfectly Self-recognized. He knows his real nature completely and in perfection. At the same time, however, this kind of intense grace cannot be resisted by his body, so he throws away his body and dies.

The second intensity of grace is called "*tīvramadhya śaktipāta*". This is "supreme-medium grace". The effect of this grace of Lord Śiva is that the recipient becomes completely and perfectly illumined but does not leave his body. He is said to be a *prātibha guru*, that is, a master who is made not by another master's initiation, but by his self, by his own grace.

The third intensity of grace is called "*tīvramanda śaktipāta*", which means "inferior supreme grace". In one who has received this grace, the desire appears for going to the feet of a spiritual master. And the master that he finds has received the second intensity of grace, *tīvramadhya śaktipāta*. This master is perfect. He is all-knowing. There is no difference between this master and Śiva.

Lord Śiva, through these three supreme intensities of grace, creates masters in the kingdom of spirituality. With lower intensities of grace, Lord Śiva creates worthy disciples.

The fourth intensity of grace is called "*madhyatīvara śaktipāta*". This is "medium-supreme grace". Through the effect of this intensity of grace, the disciple reaches the feet of that master who is absolutely perfect. But because the foundation established in the mind of this disciple is not quite completely perfect, the mere touch or glance of this perfect master will not bring this disciple to enlightenment. He, therefore, initiates this disciple in the proper fashion by giving him a *mantra* and teaching him the proper way of treading.

The fifth intensity of grace is called "*madhyamadhya śaktipāta*", which means "medium-middle grace". When Lord Śiva bestows this particular intensity of grace upon someone, the intense desire for achieving the existence of Lord Śiva arises in this person's mind. At the same time, however, he does not want to ignore the enjoyments of the world. He wants to enjoy worldly pleasure along with wanting to realize the existence of Lord Śiva. Yet the intensity of his desire is only for achieving Lord Śiva's state.

The sixth intensity of grace is called "*madhyamanda śaktipāta*", which means "medium-inferior grace." The effect of this grace is very much like the effect of medium-middle grace, however . . . the predominant desire here is for experiencing worldly pleasures.

The above three medium intensities of grace take place in the field of aspirants living in the kingdom of *śiva-dharma*. Those aspirants have the inclination to achieve the state of Self-realization at least half-hourly during the day and at least twice during the night. The remaining period they keep aside for worldly pleasures.

The following three inferior intensities of grace–*manda-tīvra* (inferior-supreme), *manda-madhya* (inferior-medium), and *manda-manda* (inferior-inferior)–take place in the field of aspirants living in *loka dharmaḥ*, the kingdom of worldly life. These aspirants have the desire for achieving Self-realization, the state of Lord Śiva, only when the pains and pressures of this world become too much to bear. At that moment, they want to abandon everything and achieve Self-realization but they are not able to, and though they want to leave this worldly life, they cannot. These aspirants have more tendency for worldly pleasure and less tendency for realizing their Self. But, as the grace of Lord Śiva shines in them, in the end–which may take many lifetimes–they become one with the supreme Being. This is the greatness of Lord Śiva's grace–that no matter what intensity of His grace is with you, it will carry you to His nature in the end.

Kashmir Shaivism–The Secret Supreme, 10.65-70.

8. The five *kalās* (circles) or *aṇḍas* (eggs).

Pṛthvi-aṇḍa, *prakṛti-aṇḍa*, *māyā-aṇḍa*, and *śakti-aṇḍa* are also known as *nivṛtti kalā*, *pratiṣṭhā kalā*, *vidyā kalā*, and *śānta kalā*, respectively. There is also a fifth circle called *śāntātītā kalā*.

Pṛthvi-aṇḍa or *nivṛtti kalā* contains the earth element. *Prakṛti-aṇḍa* or *pratiṣṭhā kalā* contains the twenty three elements from water (*jāla*) to *prakṛti*. *Māyā-aṇḍa*, or *vidyā kalā*, contains the six *kañcukas* (coverings) from *puruṣa* to *māyā*. *Śakti-aṇḍa*, or *śānta kalā*, contains four elements: *śuddhavidyā*, *īśvara*, *sadāśiva*, and *śakti*. In *śāntātītā kalā*, there is only the glamour of Lord Śiva. There is no residence of anybody [else], only this is the residence of Lord Śiva.

For further elaboration on the five *kalās* see *Kashmir Shaivism–The Secret Supreme*, 2.12.

9. *Samādhi*

The state of *samādhi* is the last limb (*aṅga*) of the eight limbs of *yoga*. The eight limbs are *yama*, *niyama*, *āsana*, *prāṇayama*, *pratyāhāra*, *dhāraṇā*, *dhyāna*, and *samādhi*. In classical *yoga* texts, the state of *samādhi* is recognized to be the hightest state, but Kashmir Shaivism treats it as a purely internal state. [*Editor's note*]

So, if you want to perceive Him, perceive the state of Lord Śiva, as it ought to be in its real sense, enjoy this universe. You will find the exact state of Lord Śiva in the universe. You won't find the real state of Lord Śiva in *samādhi*. In *samādhi*, you will find Its not-vivid formation. The vivid formation will be found only in the universal state.
Swami Lakshmanjoo, *Shiva Sutra Vimarshini*, 2.7.

When this kind of existence is experienced by such a *yogī* in the very active life of the universe, in *kriyā śakti*–not only in the state of knowledge (*jñāna śakti*), not in your internal state of consciousness of Self (*icchā śakti*), but also in the active life; in the active life also he feels and experiences the state of universal consciousness of Śiva–this is called real *samādhi* for him.
Swami Lakshmanjoo, *Shiva Sutra Vimarshini*, 3.6

10. ***Prakāśa* and *Vimarśa***

In the world of Shaivite philosophy, Lord Śiva is seen as being filled with light. But more than this, Lord Śiva is the embodiment of light and this light is different than the light of the sun, of the moon, or of fire. It is light (*prakāśa*) with Consciousness (*vimarśa*), and this light with Consciousness is the nature of that Supreme Consciousness, Lord Śiva.

What is Consciousness? The light of Consciousness is not only pure Consciousness, it is filled with the understanding that, "I am the creator, I am the protector, and I am the destroyer of everything". Just to know that, "I am the creator, I am the protector, and I am the destroyer", is Consciousness. If Consciousness was not attached to the light of Consciousness, we would have to admit that the light of the sun or the light of the moon or the light of a fire is also Lord Śiva. But this is not the case.

The light of Consciousness (*vimarśa*) is given various names. It is called *cit-caitanya*, which means, the strength of consciousness; *parā vāk,* the supreme word; *svātantrya*, perfect independence; *aiśvarya*, the predominant glory of supreme Śiva; *kartṛtva*, the power of acting; *sphurattā*, the power of existing; *sāra*, the complete essence of everything; *hṛdaya*, the universal heart; and *spanda*, universal movement. All these are names in the Tantras, which are attributed to this Consciousness.

This I-Consciousness, which is the reality of Lord Śiva, is a natural (*akṛtrima*), not a contrived, "I". It is not adjusted I-Consciousness. Limited human beings have adjusted I-Consciousness. Lord Śiva has natural or pure I-Consciousness. There is a difference between adjusted Consciousness and natural Consciousness. Adjusted or artificial consciousness exists when this I-Consciousness is attributed to your body, to your mind, to your intellect, and to your ego. Natural consciousness is that consciousness that is attributed to the reality of the Self, which is all-Consciousness.

This universe, which is created in His Consciousness, is dependent on that Consciousness. It is always dependent on that Consciousness. It cannot move outside of that Consciousness. It exists only when it is residing in His Consciousness. This is the way the creation of His universe takes place.

Self Realization in Kashmir Shaivism, 3.56-57.

There are two positions of Śiva. One is *prakāśa* and another is *vimarśa*. . . . When He feels this blissful state as His own nature, that is *prakāśa*. When He feels, "That blissful state is My glory", that is *vimarśa*. When He feels that, "This blissful state is My being", that is Śiva. When He believes that, "this is My glory", that is *śakti*. The cycle of glory is residing in *śakti*, and the cycle of *prakāśa* is residing in Śiva. Both are in one. That is indicated by *visarga* in Śiva, i.e., [the vowel] '*aḥ*' or ':'. So, *vimarśa śakti* is supreme *parā parameśvarī* attributed to *svātantrya śakti*. It is the intensity of independence of the *svātantrya* of Bhairava.

Parātriśikā Vivaraṇa, USF archives.

11. *Nirvikalpa*

In reality, everything, whatever exists, it is in *nirvikalpa* state [where] you can't define anything. . . . You can define only in the *vikalpa* state, in the cycle of *vikalpa*, e.g., when you say, "This is a specks cover". But it is not a specks cover in the real sense, in the state of God consciousness. It is just *nirvikalpa*–you can't say what it is, but it is! *Saṁketādi smaraṇam*, when you understand, "This is mine", "O, this was in my house and this is mine", this memory takes place in the *vikalpa* state, not the *nirvikalpa* state. And that *vikalpa* state cannot exist without *anubhavam*, the *nirvikalpa* state.

Nirvikalpa is the cause of all *vikalpas*; the undifferentiated state is the cause of all *vikalpas*. . . . It is not something foreign [to *vikalpas*]. It is their life. It is the life of all *vikalpas*.

Parātrīśikā Vivaraṇa, USF archives.

As long as the kingdom of God consciousness is there, there is no place for the kingdom of the mind. . . . The junk of thoughts . . . in God consciousness, they don't come. They have no right to come, they have no room to come.

DENISE: But a person who's in God consciousness and in the world, don't they have to think a thought before they perform an action?

SWAMIJI: No . . . that thought is not thought. That thought is . . . a fountain of bliss. You can't imagine unless you realize it, experience it.

JOHN: So we can't say that a man in God consciousness thinks. But he's in the world doing and acting and so many things.

SWAMIJI: But he is rolling in God consciousness. There is no worry about him. He can do everything, each and every act that an ordinary person, ignorant person, does, but for him, all is divine, all is lying in his nature (*svarūpa*).

JOHN: So thought is by its nature limited. The definition of thought is something that is limited.

SWAMIJI: Limited, yes.

JOHN: And since a man in God consciousness doesn't have limited anything, then he doesn't have thoughts.

SWAMIJI: Unlimited thought is not thought, it is *nirvikalpa*. It is the state of your own nature where there is no limitation.

Swami Lakshmanjoo, *Special Verses on Practice*, verse 65, USF archive.

12. Thirty six elements (*tattvas*)

Though Kashmir Shaivism recognises 36 *tattvas* (elements), Abhinavagupta adds an additional two states:

1) * *Mahāmāyā*: Swamiji says, "It is the gap and power of delusion. Delusion, where you won't know that you are deluded. You will conclude that you are established on truth. But that is not truth, that is not the real thing." This is the abode of the *vijñānākalas.*

2) * *Guṇa tattva*: The state where the three *guṇas* first manifest. Swamiji says, "In *prakṛti* you can't see the three *guṇas* [because] this is the seed state of the three *guṇas*. It is why in Shaivism, we have put another element . . . and that is the element of *guṇa tattva*."

Śuddha tattvas – Pure Elements

Śiva = I-ness (Being)
Śakti = I-ness (Energy of Being)
Sadāśiva = I-ness in This-ness
Īśvara = This-ness in I-ness
Śuddhavidya = I-ness in I-ness / This-ness in This-ness

Ṣaṭ kañcukas – Six Coverings

(Mahāmāyā = gap of illusion)*
Māya = illusion of individuality
Kalā = limitation of creativity/activity
Vidyā = limitation of knowledge
Rāga = limitation of attachment
Kāla = limitation of time
Niyati = limitation of place

Puruṣa = ego connected with subjectivity
Prakṛti = nature
(Guṇa tattva = manifest guṇas)*

Antaḥkaraṇas – Three Internal Organs

Buddhiḥ = intellect

Ahaṁkāra = ego connected with objectivity
Manas = mind

Pañca jñānendriyas – Five Organs of Cognition

Śrotra = ear, organ of hearing
Tvak = skin, organ of touching
Cakṣu = eye, organ of seeing
Rasanā = tongue, organ of tasting
Ghrāṇa = nose, organ of smelling

Pañca karmendriyas – Five Organs of Action

Vāk = speech
Pāṇi = hand
Pāda = foot
Pāyu = excretion
Upastha = procreative

Pañca tanmātras – Five Subtle Elements

Śabda = sound
Sparśa = touch
Rūpa = form
Rasa = taste
Gandha = smell

Pañca mahābhūtas – Five Great Elements

Ākāśa = ether
Vāyu = air
Tejas = fire
Jala = water
Pṛthvī = earth

For a full explanation of the 36 *tattvas* see *Kashmir Shaivism, The Secret Supreme*, chapter 1.

13. *Turya* and *Turyātītā*

When, by the grace of a master, this subjective body enters into subjective consciousness with full awareness, and maintaining unbroken awareness becomes fully illumined in its own Self, this is called the fourth state, *turya*.

From the Trika Shaivite point of view, predominance is given to the three energies of Śiva: *parā śakti* (the supreme energy), *parāparā śakti* (medium energy), and *aparā śakti* (inferior energy). The kingdom of *aparā śakti*, the lowest energy, is found in wakefulness and dreaming. The kingdom of *parāparā śakti*, the medium energy, is established in the state of sound sleep. And lastly, the kingdom of *parā śakti*, the supreme energy, is found in the state of *turya*.

The state of *turya* is said to be the penetration of all energies simultaneously, not in succession. All of the energies are residing there but are not in manifestation. They are all together without distinction. *Turya* is called "*savyāpārā*" because all of the energies get their power to function in that state. At the same time, this state is known as "*anāmayā*" because it remains unagitated by all of these energies.

Three names are attributed to this state; by worldly people, by *yogins*, and by illuminated humans (*jñānīs*). Worldly people call it "*turya*", which means "the fourth." They use this name because they have no descriptive name for this state. They are unaware of this state and, not having experienced it, simply call it "the fourth state". *Yogins* have attributed the name "*rūpātītā*" to this condition because this state has surpassed the touch of one's self and is the establishment of one's Self. The touch of one's self was found in sound sleep, however, the establishment of one's Self takes place in *turya*. For illuminated humans, *jñānīs*, the entire universal existence is found in this state of *turya*, collectively, as undifferentiated, in the state of totality. There is no succession here. *Jñānīs*, therefore, call this state "*pracaya*", the undifferentiated totality of universal existence.

Turyātīta is that state which is the absolute fullness of Self. It is filled with all-consciousness and bliss. It is really the last and the supreme state of the Self. You not only find this state of *turyātīta* in *samādhi*, you also find it in each and every activity of the world. In this state, there is no possibility for the practice of *yoga*. If you can practice *yoga*, then you are not in *turyātīta*. In practicing *yoga*, there is the intention of going somewhere. Here, there is nowhere to go, nothing to achieve. As concentration does not exist here, the existence of the helping hand of *yoga* is not possible.

There are only two names actually attributed to this state of *turyātīta*, one given by worldly people and one by *jñānīs*. Worldly people, because they know nothing about the state, call it "*turyātītā*", which means "that state which is beyond the fourth". *Jñānīs*, on the other hand, also have a name for it. They call it "*mahāpracaya*", which means "the unlimited and unexplainable supreme totality". *Yogins* do not actually attribute any name to this state because they have no knowledge of it. It is completely outside of their experience. *Yogins* have though, through the use of their imagination and guesswork, imagined one name which might be apropriate for this state: "*satatoditam*", which means "that state which has no pause, no break". It is a breakless and unitary state. In *samādhi*, It is there. When *samādhi* is absent, It is there. In the worldly state, It is there. In the dreaming state, It is there. And in the state of deep sleep, It is there. In each and every state of the individual subjective body, It is there.

Kashmir Shaivism–The Secret Supreme, 11.72-84.

The difference between *turya* and *turyātīta* is, in *turya*, you find in *samādhi* that this whole universe is existing there in the seed form, germ. The strength, the energy, of universal existence is existing there . . . but here he has [yet] to come out [into activity]. In *turyātīta*, he comes out in action and feels universal consciousness. This is the difference between *turya* and *turyātīta*.

Tantrāloka 10.288, USF archive.

14. **Spanda System**

The fourth system which comprises the Trika philosophy is called the Spanda system. The word *spanda* means "movement". The Spanda school recognizes that nothing can exist without movement. Where there is movement, there is life, and where there is no movement, that is lifelessness. They realize that there is movement in wakefulness, dreaming, deep sleep, and *turya*. Though some thinkers argue that there is no movement in deep sleep, the philosophers of the Spanda system realize that nothing can exist without movement.

The teachings of the Spanda system, which is an important practical system, are found embodied in the *Vijñāna Bhairava*

Tantra, the *Svacchanda Tantra*, and in the 6th chapter of the *Tantrāloka*.
Kashmir Shaivism–The Secret Supreme, 19.134.

Spanda is nominated as *sphurattā* (vigor, life, life-giver, power of existence), *ūrmiḥ* (tide), *balam* (strength), *udyoga* (force), *hṛdayam* (heart), *sāram* (essence), and *mālinī* (supreme energy). These are nominations which are attributed to this *spanda* in the *śāstras*.
Swami Lakshmanjoo, *Spanda Saṁdoha* of Kṣemarāja, USF archive.

The one who is always completely aware to apprehend the essence of *spanda* in each and every movement of life quickly gains entry in God consciousness in the very state of wakefulness.
Spanda Kārikā 1.21.

This universe, which is a world of consciousness, is filled with and is one with the supreme state of God conscious-ness. God consciousness is *spanda*, a unique reality of su-preme movement filled with nectar and an outpouring of the supreme bliss of independence.
Shiva Sutra–The Supreme Awakening, 1.9.

The element of *spanda* is that being of God consciousness in which this whole universe exists and from which this whole universe comes out . . . And [God consciousness] is not only the resting place of the universe, this is the *prasara sthana* also, the flowing energy. This universe comes out from That . . . it *has* to exist in God consciousness and it is coming out from God consciousness *in* God consciousness, because there is no other space for the universe to exist.
Parātrīśikā Vivaraṇa, USF archive.

Just [examine] your cycle of organs (*karaṇavargaḥ*). . . . This *karaṇavargaḥ* is *vimūḍhaḥ*, is dead, is lifeless. . . . If it were not lifeless, what has happened to these [organs] in a dead body? All his organs are okay but he can't see, he can't hear, he can't feel the sensation of touch, he can't smell, he can't do anything. . . .

And from which power this dead cycle of organs *amūḍhavat*, become just as if it is filled with life? *Spanda* is installed in it and then it becomes life-full.

The state of wakefulness, the state of dreaming state, and the state of dreamless state . . . can't remain, it can't exist in the outside cycle of the world without *spanda* . . . because *spanda* is the life for this world.

Swami Lakshmanjoo, *Spanda Kārikā* audio, USF archive.

15. ***Pramiti, pramātṛ, pramāṇa, prameya bhava.***

Pramiti bhava is the supreme subjective state, *pramātṛ bhava* is the pure subjective state, *pramāṇa bhava* is the cognitive state, and *prameya bhava* is the objective state.

There is difference between *pramātṛ bhāva* and *pramiti bhāva*. *Pramātṛi bhāva* is that state of consciousness where objective perception is attached. When that state of *pramātṛ bhāva* is attached with objective perception, that is pure state of *pramātṛ bhāva*. When it moves to the state where there is no objective perception, there is no touch of objective perception, it is beyond objective perception, that is *pramiti bhāva*. Swami Lakshmanjoo, *Tantrāloka* 4.124, commentary, USF archive.

[*Pramiti bhāva* is an] objectless-subjective state. It is residing in only pure subjective consciousness. It has nothing to do with the object. When there is the objective state also attached to the subjective state, that is not *pramiti bhāva*, that is *pramātṛ bhāva*. And when that objective state is connected with the cognitive state, that is *pramāṇa bhāva*. When that objective state is completely a pure objective state, that is *prameya bhāva*. And *pramiti bhāva* is complete subjective consciousness without the slightest touch and trace of this object. In the long run, everything resides in *pramiti bhāva*; *pramiti bhāva* is the life of all the three. This is pure consciousness. . . . And that *pramiti bhāva* is absolutely one with *svātantrya śakti* . . . it is one with Lord Śiva.

Swami Lakshmanjoo, *Tantrāloka* 11.72-73a, USF archive.

In fact, this *pramiti bhāva* is the real source of understanding anything. Whatever you see, it must touch the state of *pramiti bhāva*, otherwise you won't understand it. For instance, you see [an object]. You'll only know [that object] when this sensation of [that object already] resides in *pramiti bhāva*, in that super state of subjective consciousness. And the super state of subjective consciousness is not differentiated. From that undifferentiated point of *pramiti bhāva*, the differentiated flow of *pramātṛ bhāva* and *pramāṇa bhāva* flow out. Swami Lakshmanjoo, *Tantrāloka* 11.62, USF archive.

It is *nirvikalpa*, it is a thoughtless state. And in that thoughtless state, it [i.e., all knowledge] must reside, otherwise it is not known. It will be unknown for . . . eternity. Ibid. 11.68-69.

For instance, when you are [giving a lecture while] reading your book, your consciousness is *with* an object. When you are giving a lecture without a book, without any support, your consciousness is *without* an object, it flows out . . . this is the state of *pramiti bhāva*. Swami Lakshmanjoo, *Tantrāloka* 6.180, USF archive.

Appendix B

Paramārthasāra, with Yogarājas commentary, translation John Hughes, Ishwar Ashram, Srinagar Kashmir, 1972. (PhD. thesis, McMaster University, Hamilton, Ontario.)

1. O Śaṁbhu, thou art the supreme (the one) who is abiding above the abyss (of *māyā*), He who is beginning-less. (Thou art the one) who has entered into the many caves (i.e., the hearts). Thou art thus the abode of all as thou art dwelling in everything (whether it be animate or inanimate.) (To thee alone) I approach for refuge.

2. The disciple, bewildered by the wheel of suffering which begins with life in the womb and ends in death, asks the guru, blessed *Ādhāra*, for Truth.

3. The guru (*Ādhāra*) declared to him the essence of Truth (lit. *Paramārthasāra*) in the (form) of the *Ādhāra kārikās*. Abhinavagupta declares that (essence of Truth) in accordance with the viewpoint of the teaching.

4. Through the brimming fullness of the power of His own energy has been produced separately these four spheres (egg shaped circles) and they are *śakti, māyā, prakṛti*, and *pṛthvī*.

5. In all this universe which is the continuum of diverse bodies, organs, worlds, therein the enjoyer is Śiva, embodied, having assumed the condition of the unaware.

6. Just as a flawless crystal takes to itself the forms of various colors so likewise the Lord too assumes the forms of gods, men, animals, trees, etc.

7. Just as the reflected orb of the moon moves when the water (in which it is being reflected) moves, and does not move when

(this water) does not move so, likewise this Self who is the supreme Self (shows itself) in the aggregate of bodies, organs and worlds.

8. Just as Rāhu although invisible appears when he is in the orb of the moon. So likewise this Self although omnipresent (appears) upon the mirror of the intellect through contact with the objects of senses.

9. Just as a face appears upon a mirror which is free from dirt so likewise this (Self) which is light itself appears in the *tattva* of the intellect which is pure by reason of the grace (*śaktipāta*) of Śiva.

10-11. The universe which is thirty six fold shines within that which is the supreme *tattva*, which is light, replete, experiencing the greatest bliss because of the resting in Himself, overflowing with the instruments of his conscious will. He is full with infinite energies free from all discursiveness (*vikalpa*), pure, at rest, without emergence of recession.

12-13. Just as a manifold consisting of a town, a village etc., appears without being separate upon the surface of a mirror and yet at the same time appears as divided within itself and from that (awareness).

So this universe also appears as void of distinction from the absolutely pure supreme awareness of Bhairava and at the same time appears as divided within itself and from that (awareness).

14. He (Paramaśiva) reveals as separate from Himself the *tattvas* of the five *śaktis* (energies) (*cit, ānanda, icchā, jñāna, kriyā*) which are *śiva, śakti, sadāśiva, īśvara*, and *vidyā*.

15. The supreme freedom of the Lord is able to accomplish the seemingly impossible and this is the self concealment of Śiva by the goddess who is *māyā śakti*.

16. Consciousness, being soiled through taking upon itself *māyā* becomes *puruṣa*, the limited subject. (*Puruṣa*) is bound by

the force of time, limited creativity, limitation, attachment, and limited knowledge, (*kāla, kalā, niyati, rāga, vidya*).

17. "Now this is just something that I know fully." Along with *māyā* this forms that six-fold shroud (*kañcuka*) and these are said to be the inner limbs of the limited being.

18. Just as the husk, though separate, is established in the rice grain as one with it, (so the set of six *kañcukas*), though in one sense separate from the individual, are established as one with him. However, the six *kañcukas* become purified by means of turning toward the path of Śiva.

19. (First) *prakṛti* (nature) which is nothing but pleasure, pain, and delusion, and then the internal organs which are successively *buddhi, mana*, and *ahaṁkāra* (discrimination, thought, and egoity) appear because there takes place judgement (*niścayaḥ*), thought (*saṁkalpa*) and pride (*abhimāna*).

20. Ear (*śrotram*), the skin (*tvak*), the eye (*akṣi*), the tongue (*rasanā*), the nose (*ghrāṇam*), these are the organs of intellection (and have) sound etc., (as their objects). Furthermore the organs of action are the hand (*pāṇi*), mouth (*vāk*), the foot (*pāda*), the organs of excretion (*pāyu*), and the organs of generation (*upastha*).

21. That subtle objective field which would be without objective qualification, that is the pentad of the *tanmātras* which are (*śabda*) sound, (*sparśa*) touch sensation, (*rūpa*) form, (*rasa*) flavor, (*gandha*) smell.

22. However, by the force of the mingling of these (*tanmātras*) the gross objects (of knowledge and action) become the elements ether, air, fire, water and earth.

23. Just as the husk covers the rice grain so creation, beginning with *prakṛti* and ending with earth, conceals consciousness with the physical state.

24. Here the supreme covering is *mala*, the subtle shroud is that which begins with *māyā*, and the gross shroud is the external in the form of objects, for the Self is enshrouded by three encasings.

25. (The Self) because it has come into contact with that darkness of ignorance would be aware of its essential Self in the various diversity of objects and subjects.

26. Just as syrup, brown sugar, molasses, and purified sugar are just the juice of the sugar cane, so all these different conditions are Śambu, the supreme Self.

27. *Vijñāna, antaryāmi, prāṇa, virāt, deha, jāti*, and *piṇḍa*, etc., these have only a practical reality (*vyavahāra*). From the point of view of the ultimate in reality they do not exist.

28. There is no snake in the rope (and yet when taken as a snake) it causes fear even ending in death. The great power of illusion (*bhrānti*) cannot be understood.

This he validates in the subject at hand.

29. Likewise pain, pleasure, birth, death, heaven, hell, right and wrong, the castes, the stages of life etc., although in the Self they have no real existence, i.e., they exist by the force of delusion.

30. So this darkness is considering things as not Self when in reality they are not separate from the Self because they appear.

31. This is darkness upon darkness, this is that great pimple on the boil, that there is the false conception of Self in the body, life principle (*prāṇa*) etc., although they are not the Self.

32. In wondrous ways he wraps himself about with the sphere of the awareness of the body, breath, intellectual knowledge, the voids, just like a spider with its own web.

33. By means of the revelation of the power of Self-knowledge, uncovering his own Self, in this fashion Paramaśiva manifests that sport (which is at one moment) diverse with binding and (then again) liberating.

34. Creation, preservation and destruction, the waking state, the dreaming state, and deep sleep shine in that fourth abode. (And even then) it (this fourth abode) shines as unconcealed by them.

35. The waking state is called "*viśvaya*" because of diversity. The sleeping state is called "*tejaḥ*" because of the greatness of its illumination. The state of deep sleep is called the "*prājña*" because of the compactness of knowledge therein. Beyond that is the fourth.

36. Just as the surface of the sky is not soiled by smoke, clouds, or dust. So likewise the supreme subject is not touched by the transformations of *māyā*.

37. (Just as) when the air contained in a single pot is full of dust other portions of air contained within pots do not become dirtied, so likewise, these limited individuals who enjoy the diversity of happiness and unhappiness.

38. (When the aggregate of *tattvas*) is at rest this Lord seems as if at rest. (When it is) delighted (He seems as if) delighted. (When it is) confused (He seems as if) confused. But he is not really so.

39. First having rejected the projection of the Self into the not Self, then the supreme Self destroys the delusion of no Self in the Self.

40. For the supreme yogi who has succeeded in cutting out (along) with the root this pair of illusions. For him there is no thought at all of anything else to be done.

41. This triad, earth, *prakṛti*, and *māyā*, which has fallen into objectivity becomes nothing but pure Being through the force of

the realization of non-duality.

42. Just as a girdle, an earring and a bracelet are seen as gold and nothing else when the distinction between them is abandoned. Likewise, when diversity is abandoned then everything appears as pure being.

43. This brahman who is supreme, pure, quiescent, non-dual, unvarying, universal, the real nectar, (He) rests in effulgent *śakti* whose nature is light (*bhā*).

44. Whatever is not realized by that awareness whose nature is light, (which takes the form of) it is willed, it is known, and it is done, that is just like a sky flower.

45. This whole universe is created (emitted) by the God of gods through coming into contact with the trident of *śaktis* (*icchā, jñāna* and *kriyā*) in that reality known as *śiva*.

46. And once again this triad of spheres is created outside also in the process of pouring forth of the five *śaktis* (energies by objectifying) the Self.

47. Thus I alone, God, propel the device of the wheel of *śaktis*, standing as the controller of the great wheel of *śaktis*.

48. In me alone the universe shines like objects in an unspotted mirror. The universe emerges from me like the diversity of a dream from the (state of) deep sleep.

49. I alone am the universe, like a body consists of hands, feet, etc. And I alone flash forth as this universe like the nature of light in things.

50. I am the seer, I am the hearer, I am the smeller, although I am without bodily organs. And although I am not their composer yet I alone create the various schools, scriptures, and philosophical arguments.

51. Thus when dualistic thought is melted, transcending

deluding *māyā,* he would be dissolved in brahman like water into water and milk into milk.

52. And when the aggregate of *tattvas* has thus become integrated into Śiva through awareness then what grief or what delusion could be for one beholding the universe as brahman?

53. Right and wrong, the fruit of action, arises simply as a result of false knowledge and attachment, for the fault of association is difficult to overcome just like the association with a thief by a man who is not a thief.

54. Those who, in this life, in delusion, resort to that ignorance which is produced by the practical reality (*vyavahāra*) of the world, they experience birth and death bound by the chains of right and wrong.

55. Yet action which consists of right and wrong gathered in the time of ignorance is destroyed, like down (cotton) which has been stored for a long time, by the force of the blazing brilliance of enlightenment (*vijñana*).

56. In the attainment of enlightenment his acts do not bear fruit therefore how can there be birth for him. Since the bondage of birth has departed from him he shines as the sun with his own rays, free of the bondage of birth, in the form of Śiva.

57. Just as a seed which is without its internal kernel, external kernel, and involcure, does not produce a sprout, so likewise the Self cannot produce the sprout of existence when it is freed of *āṇava, māyīya* and *karma mala*.

58. The knower of the Self is afraid of nothing for everything everywhere is his own form. Nor does he grieve for there is no destruction in the Real.

59. Because of the hoard of jewels of reality (which is the awareness) "I alone exist" which are amassed in the most secret treasure house of the heart, who could suffer what poverty in this state of the Lord?

60. There is no abode of liberation (*mokṣa*) nor is there any going to some other place. Liberation (*mokṣa*) is the manifesting of ones own power through the severing of the knot of ignorance.

61. This man in whom the knot of ignorance has been severed, in whom all doubt has disappeared and error has been conquered, in whom both merit and demerit have been destroyed, he is released even though he is still one with his body.

62. Just as a seed which has been burnt by fire becomes incapable of growing a sprout, so also action which has been burnt by the fire of knowledge cannot be the cause for rebirth.

63. Because of the limited intellect and through the mental projection of a future body which is appropriate to his actions (*karma*), awareness becomes contracted and when this body is destroyed it (awareness) also becomes so.

64-65-66. But if one were to realize the Self which is one with Śiva, that is, as unspotted awareness which is the knower and the doer, transcending the universe, infinite, whose form is light which neither arises nor sets, whose every desire is fulfilled; which is free of the determinations of space and time, which is firm, undying, lordly, completely full, the sole agent that brings about the disposition of the creation and destruction of the multitude of the countless energies, which is the skillful performance of creation etc.,–then how indeed could it be that one is in *saṁsāra*, i.e., whence or wither can the infinite go?

67. So (as it has been established) by logical arguments that the act of the enlightened man, which has already taken place, does not bear fruit, for through the firm conviction, "this is not for me but for Him", there is no fruit in the world.

68. Thus awakened by the wind of cultivated awareness he sacrificing all thoughts in the brilliance of his Self becomes nothing but that brilliance.

69. Eating whatever comes his way, clad with any garment, tranquil, dwelling in any place, he is released. He who is all

beings (and is the Self of all beings).

70. Though he does hundreds of thousands of horse sacrifices, even though he performs hundreds of thousands of murders of brahmans, since he knows reality he is not touched either by merits or by sins. He is not touched at all in his purity.

71. Avoiding passion, delight, anger, desire, melancholy, fear, greed, delusion, free from hymns or sacrificial mantras (*vaṣaṭ*) he would live like one lifeless, with a mind free of arguments.

72. This collection of passion, delight, etc., holds sway because of the illusion of duality. How indeed could he who has attained the awareness of his undivided Self be touched by that?

73. There is nothing separate from him to be praised or to be sacrificed to. Nor would the enlightened man delight in such things as hymns. Therefore he is free from all forms of obeisance and mantra.

74. His temple is his own or another body, supported by the thirty-six *tattvas*. It is complete with windows which are the arrangements of the (apertures) of the senses of the body.)

75. United with his energies he is established, worshipping the auspicious deity which is the supreme Bhairava of his supreme Self, with substances which are pure through Self awareness.

76. The sacrifice into the extremely brilliant fire of consciousness takes place without effort for him who offers the mass of the great seed of diversity which is external and internal conception.

77. Meditation (*dhyānam*) is ceaseless for this Lord manifests various forms. That alone is meditation in which reality is painted (on the canvas) of the mind.

78. In as much as he causes to revolve in inner awareness, the whole sequence of the world, and the delineation of the sequence of the *tattvas*, and the assembly of the senses, this is said to be his *japa* (repetition of *mantra*).

79-80. This is his oath which is both difficult and easy, that he sees everything with equal vision and that he realizes his awareness to delight in the cremation ground of the universe. And (also) that he conceives awareness as marked by the conception of the corpse which is the body. And (furthermore) he relishes the skull which is the sphere of the known which rests in the rays of his own senses and which is filled with the intoxicating liquor which is the liquid essence of the universe.

81. Thus realizing that which is called Maheśvara, the absolute, which is free from birth and death, by the grace of the light of the nature of the perceiver, he remains, all his needs fulfilled, in accordance with his desires.

82. He whomever knows the supreme and unparalleled bliss, which is all-pervading, which has (previously) been realized in this way, which is identical with everything, and which has thrown off all diversity, he becomes one with That.

83. Abandoning his body in a holy place or in the house of an untouchable, even though he may have lost all memory, released at the moment of his enlightenment, he proceeds to absolute Self identity (*kaivalyam*), all suffering destroyed.

84. Frequenting *tirthas* (shrines) bestows merit, dying in the house of an untouchable leads to hell. But that means nothing when there is no contact with the limitation of good and evil.

85-86. The placing of a grain of rice which has been properly separated from its two husks (back) into the segments of the husks does not enable that (grain) of rice to return to its original state. Likewise consciousness (*saṁvit*) separated from the collection of the shrouds (*kañcukas*) although remaining here (in this collection) by the force of latent traces being essentially liberated is unaffected by it.

87-88. Just like a jewel in which purity has been fashioned by the most skillful craftsmen, though it becomes dirty when it is in contact with its case, is really pure once one removes these contingent factors (*upādhiḥ*).

So (also) that awareness which is free of the establishment of impurity through the teaching of the spiritual master being liberated from the limitations of the body shines as Śiva, as absolutely void of limitations.

89. So he, on the authority of scripture etc., or through unswerving faith, attaining identity therewith in life (subsequently) will attain heaven, hell or human birth.

90-91. But the 'last moment' of this man, which is favoring a righteous or sinful estate, seems to the stupid to be a cooperating cause. But (yet) it is not a cause for transmigration.

And even those who by identifying therewith went to their various estates as animals, birds, reptiles, etc., even they attain that state purified by former knowledge.

92-93. So this soul rests in the state between assuming physical forms as heaven or as hell. And when that (*karma*) is exhausted he is united with another body in accordance with his own fitness.

But that Self which was revealed on the occasion of knowledge, It, at the time of death, is in exactly the same state as it was realized to be (at the occasion of the revelation of knowledge.)

94-95. The complete occlusion of the aggregate of the organic functions, the destruction of memory, the choking of the breath, the breaking in the vital parts, specific ailments, the experience which comes from the impressions of the body, how could this not be when there is union with the body? Yet even though he is unconscious at the moment of death the enlightened man (*jñāni*) does not fall from the reality of his own Self.

96. When from the mouth of the Guru one reaches the path of the supreme reality, so just then, instantaneously there is the descent of the most high Grace (*śaktipāta*) and Śiva is without obscuration.

97. Abiding as the All-transcending form, because of the stages (*krama*) which are like stages of refuge, having risen to gain the highest *tattva*, at last he becomes the fullness of Śiva.

98-99. Of that yogi who has not attained the state of the fullness of the supreme reality but is resting in the center, or of that one who is eager to gain that place of refuge but has gone astray from yoga (*yoga bhraṣṭa*), and having that consciousness would at some time die, then as it is said in the *śāstras*, he will be the Lord of the amazing enjoyments of the world of the gods. And from the influence of resting at that state, in the next birth (*janma*) he attains the state of Śiva.

100. Verily he though not attaining that practice of yoga which is the path to the supreme reality, yet being the enjoyer of the enjoyments of heaven, happy minded, he is happy for a long time.

101. As the universal emperor of all particulars is worshipped as a king by all people, so he who has fallen from yoga is worshipped in the worlds of heaven by all deities.

102. After a long time he again attains the existence of man and practicing yoga he obtains the heavenly nectar (which is *mokṣa*) and therefore does not return again.

103. Therefore he whosoever is bent upon treading upon this path of reality, he attains to Śiva-ness. So knowing this, he should attempt to gain that supreme reality by any and every means.

104. This meditating upon highest Brahman, he instantaneously reaches Śiva-ness by abiding in his own heart. As is made manifest briefly by Abhinavagupta.

105. This essence of *śāstra* which is very deep is concisely put by me Abhinavagupta in 100 *ślokas*, remembering Śiva's rays by which I am lighted.

Bibliography

Swami Lakshmanjoo - Published text

Bhagavad Gita in the Light of Kashmir Shaivism (with original video), Swami Lakshmanjoo, ed. John Hughes (Universal Shaiva Fellowship, Los Angeles, 2013), xxi, 683.

Kashmir Shaivism, The Secret Supreme, Swami Lakshmanjoo, ed. John Hughes (Universal Shaiva Fellowship, Los Angeles, 1985-2003).

Self Realization in Kashmir Shaivism, The Oral Teachings of Swami Lakshmanjoo, ed. John Hughes (State University of New York Press, Albany, 1995).

Śivastotrāvalī of Utpaladevācaryā With the Sanskrit commentary of Kṣemarāja, edited with Hindi commentary by Rājānaka Lakṣmaṇa (Swami Lakshmanjoo) (Chowkhamba Sanskrit Series 15. Varanasi, 1964).

Festival of Devotion and Praise, Shivastotravali, Hymns to Shiva by Utpaladeva, Swami Lakshmanjoo, ed. John Huges, (Universal Shaiva Fellowship, Los Angeles, 2014).

Shiva Sutras, The Supreme Awakening, Swami Lakshmanjoo, ed. John Hughes (Universal Shaiva Fellowship, Los Angeles, 2002).

Vijñāna Bhairava, The Manual for Self Realization, Swami Lakshmanjoo, ed. John Hughes (Universal Shaiva Fellowship, Los Angeles, 2007).

Swami Lakshmanjoo - Unpublished texts (USF archives)

Bhagavad Gitartha Samgraha of Abhinavagupta, translation and commentary by Swami Lakshmanjoo (original audio recording, USF archives, Los Angeles, 1978).

Interview on Kashmir Shaivism, Swami Lakshmanjoo with Alexis Sanderson and John Hughes (original audio recordings, USF archives, Los Angeles 1980).

Janmamaraṇavicāragranthaḥ, Janma Maraṇa Vicāra of Bhaṭṭa Vāmadeva, Swami Lakshmanjoo (original audio recording, USF archives, Los Angeles, 1980).

Kashmir Shaivism, The Secret Supreme, Swami Lakshmanjoo (original audio recording, USF archives, Los Angeles, 1972).

Paramārthasāra of Abhinavagupta, with the commentary of Yogarāja, translation and commentary by Swami Lakshmanjoo (original video recording, USF archives, Los Angeles, 1990).

Parātriśikā Laghuvṛtti with the commentary of Abhinavagupta, translation and commentary by Swami Lakshmanjoo (original audio recording, USF archives, Los Angeles, 1982).

Parātriśikā Vivaraṇa with the commentary of Abhinavagupta, translation and commentary by Swami Lakshmanjoo (original audio recording, USF archives, Los Angeles, 1982-85).

Śivastotrāvalī of Utpaladeva, translation and commentary by Swami Lakshmanjoo (additional audio recording, USF archives, Los Angeles, 1975-80).

Spanda Kārikā of Vasugupta with the Nirṇaya (commentary) of Kṣemarāja, translation and commentary by Swami Lakshmanjoo (original audio recording, USF archives, Los Angeles, 1975).

Spanda Saṁdoha of Kṣemarāja, translation and commentary by Swami Lakshmanjoo (original audio recording, USF archives, Los Angeles, 1981).

Stava Cintāmaṇi of Bhaṭṭanārāyaṇa, translation and commentary by Swami Lakshmanjoo (original audio recording, USF archives, Los Angeles, 1980-81).

The Tantrāloka of Abhinavagupta, Chapters 1 to 18, translation and commentary by Swami Lakshmanjoo (original audio recording, USF archives, Los Angeles, 1972-1981).

Vātūlanātha Sūtras of Anantaśaktipāda, translation and commentary by Swami Lakshmanjoo (original audio recordings, USF archives, Los Angeles, 1979).

Additional sources - Books

The Paramārthasāra by Abhinava Gupta, with commentary of Yogarāja. Kashmir Series of Texts and Studies, ed. by Jagdisha Chandra Chatterji B.A. The research Department of The Kashmir State, Vol. VII, Srinagar, Kashmir, 1916.

Paramārthasāra, with Yogarājas commentary, translation John Hughes, Ishwar Ashram, Srinagar Kashmir, 1972. (PhD. thesis, McMaster University, Hamilton, Ontario.)

Pratyabhijñāhṛdayam, The Secret of Self-Recognition, Sanskrit Text with English Translation, Notes and Introduction by Jaideva Singh (Motilal Banarsidass, Delhi, 1963-2011).

Paramārthasāra of Ādi Śeṣa. S.S. Suryanarayana Sastri, (California: Asian Humanities Press, 2003.)

Yoga: Immortality and Freedom, Mircea Eliade, trans. Willard R. Trask (Princeton: Princeton University Pres, 1969.)

The Bhagavad Gītā, Winthrop Sargeant, (Albany: State University of New York Press, 1994.)

The Doctrine of the Mālinīvijayottaratantra (Alexis Sanderson) in *Ritual and Speculation in Early Tantrism. Studies in Honor of Andre Padoux,* ed. T. Goudriaan (Albany: State University of New York Press 1992.)

Doctrine of Divine Recognition, K.C. Pandey (Delhi: Motilal Banarsidass, 1986.)

Spanda Kārikās – The Divine Creative Pulsation. Jaideva Singh, (Delhi: Motilal Banarsidass, 1980), 167.

The Scientific Foundations of Jainism. Mardia, K.V. (Delhi: Motilal Banarsidass Publishers, 1996.)

The Canon of the Śaivāgama and the Kubjika Tantras of the Western Kaula Tradition. Mark S.G. Dyczkowski, (New York: State University of New York Press, 1988).

path 145
penetrate 155
perception 142, 145
philosophy 150, 156
play 141, 143
power 141, 151, 155, 157
practice 155
prakāśaḥ 150–151
pralayākala 145
pramātṛ 145–146
prameya 145
prasara 157
predominance 155
protector 150
pure 141, 150–151
purity 143
puruṣa 139
question 146
reality 146, 151, 157
realization 141
reside 142, 147
rest 147
rūpātītā 155
Sadāśiva 146
sakalā 145
śaktiḥ 141–142, 151, 155
śaktopāya 147
samādhi 155–156
śāmbhavopāya 147
Saṁdoha 157
sāra 151
sāram 157
śāstra 157
second 145
secret 138, 142, 146–147, 149, 156–157
seed 156
self 141, 146, 151, 154–155
sense 142–143, 152
Shaivaite 150, 155
Shaivism 138, 141–142, 146–147, 149, 151, 156–157
Shiva 157
simultaneously 155
sleep 145, 155–156
sound 155
sovereignty 146
space 157
spanda 151, 156–157
specks 152
sphurattā 151, 157
spiritual 145
sthana 157
strength 147, 150, 156–157
subjective 145, 154, 156
succession 155
śuddhavidyā 146
Sun 150
support 147
supreme 138, 142, 146–147, 149–151, 155–157
Sūtra 157
svarūpaṁ 143
svātantrya 141–143, 145–146, 151
system 156
Tantrāloka 143, 156–157

Teachings of Swami Lakshmanjoo published by The Lakshmanjoo Academy

Bhagavad Gita, In the Light of Kashmir Shaivism

Festival of Devotion & Praise, Hymns to Shiva
Shivastotravali by Utpaladeva

Vijñāna Bhairava, The Manual for Self Realization

Revelations on Grace and Spiritual Practice

Shiva Sutras, The Supreme Awakening

Kashmir Shaivism, The Secret Supreme

Self Realization in Kashmir Shaivism,
The Oral Teachings of Swami Lakshmanjoo

The teachings of Swami Lakshmanjoo are a response to the urgent need of our time: the transformation of consciousness and the evolution of a more enlightened humanity.

The Universal Shaiva Fellowship and its educational branch, The Lakshmanjoo Academy, a fully accredited non-profit organization, was established under Swamij's direct inspiration, for the purpose of realizing Swamiji's vision of making Kashmir Shaivism available to the whole world. It was Swamiji's wish that his teachings be made available without the restriction of caste, creed or color. The Universal Shaiva Fellowship and the Lakshmanjoo Academy have preserved Swamiji's original teachings and are progressively making these teachings available in book, audio and video formats.

This knowledge is extremely valuable and uplifting for all of humankind. It offers humanity a clear and certain vision in a time of uncertainty. It shows us the way home and gives us the means for its attainment.

For information on Kashmir Shaivism or to support the work of The Universal Shaiva Fellowship and the Lakshmanjoo Academy and its profound consciousness work,

visit the Lakshmanjoo Academy website or
email us at info@LakshmanjooAcademy.org.

www.LakshmanjooAcademy.org

Instructions to download audio files

1. Open this link to download the free audio . . .
   https://www.universalshaivafellowship.org/Essence

   It will **direct** you to "**Essence of the Supreme Reality - Audio**".

2. Select "**Add to basket** " which will send you to the next page.

3. Copy "**Essence**" into the "**Add Gift Certificate or Coupon"** box

4. Click "**Checkout**" and fill in your details to process the free downloads.

   If you have any difficulties please contact us at:
   www.LakshmanjooAcademy.org/contact

11886476R00119

Printed in Great Britain
by Amazon.co.uk, Ltd.,
Marston Gate.